WARRING
with WISDOM

DESTINY IMAGE BOOKS BY DAWNA DE SILVA

Prayers, Declarations, and Strategies for Shifting Atmospheres

Shifting Atmospheres (TP & Curriculum)

Sozo (with Teresa Liebscher)

WARRING
with WISDOM

YOUR STRATEGY FOR VICTORIOUS SPIRITUAL WARFARE:
BODY, SOUL, & SPIRIT

DAWNA DE SILVA

DESTINY IMAGE® PUBLISHERS, INC.

P.O. Box 310, Shippensburg, PA 17257-0310

"Promoting Inspired Lives."

This book and all other Destiny Image and Destiny Image Fiction books are available at Christian bookstores and distributors worldwide.

Cover design by Eileen Rockwell
Interior design by Terry Clifton

For more information on foreign distributors, call 717-532-3040.

Reach us on the Internet: www.destinyimage.com.

ISBN 13 TP: 978-0-7684-5428-4
ISBN 13 eBook: 978-0-7684-5429-1
ISBN 13 HC: 978-0-7684-5431-4
ISBN 13 LP: 978-0-7684-5430-7

For Worldwide Distribution, Printed in the U.S.A.

1 2 3 4 5 6 7 8 / 24 23 22 21 20

DEDICATION

FOR THOSE READY TO BATTLE.

Acknowledgments

As with any book, *Warring with Wisdom* enlisted the help of many collaborators. The first of these is Stephen, my husband and champion of forty years. All the revelations he has gleaned from God, openly shared with me, and allowed me to put in this manuscript have helped my quest in understanding spiritual warfare immensely. Secondly, my son, Cory, has partnered with me to produce all five of my published books. Little did I know that when Steve and I sent him off to college he would become one of my greatest assets in putting my words to print. Thirdly, I would like to thank all the pastoral leaders at Bethel Church who have each laid a foundation of authority on which I can build. Fourthly, my Redding, California-based Transformation Center team who daily equips others to win their own battles against the enemy. And lastly, to all my Sozo peeps who are stationed in their various cities around the world, without your support, this book (and all the others) would have remained sermon notes.

AUTHOR'S NOTE

The stories in this book, while faithfully representing each account of a person's freedom, have been modified to protect the person's identity. Otherwise, they represent real people in authentic situations.

CONTENTS

INTRODUCTION

BORN FOR WAR

We are human, but we don't
wage war as humans do.
—2 Corinthians 10:3 NLT

As an inner healing and deliverance minister, I get to teach often about the subject of spiritual warfare. Over the years, I have had the privilege of reminding people it is really all about perspective. When we believe the enemy is stronger than God, we battle from a place of fear. Yet when we look at Scripture, we can clearly see that because of Christ's death and resurrection, our victorious position in this battle is being seated with Jesus in the heavenlies.

If you have been a Christian for any length of time, you have probably already heard a sermon or two on the subject of spiritual warfare. You may have even read some books or attended Bible studies that covered the topic. For you veterans of spiritual warfare, I pray you find some fresh insights in these pages and use them to do battle more wisely.

If you are new to the subject, I'll state the idea of spiritual warfare simply. Spiritual warfare, in its most basic terms, is the biblical concept of a cosmic war of good versus evil. It is the attack against us (God's children) by the enemy of our souls, satan. How we win this war depends greatly on our ability to take our focus off what the enemy is doing and to place it on God's goodness where it belongs.

In my second book, *Shifting Atmospheres*, we explored the idea of discerning and displacing spiritual atmospheres. I believe the spiritual realm—the unseen dimension—gives off certain broadcasts or messages that can either be in accordance with God's will or at war against it. By identifying what the enemy is saying and partnering with God to magnify His broadcasts instead, we can learn how to become catalysts for transforming the world around us. In this book, *Warring with Wisdom*, we will look at many ways we can war victoriously in the spiritual realm.

By the end of this book you will be better equipped to understand what types of spiritual battles are going on around you. You will be able to use practical and biblical tools to renounce and reverse the enemy's attacks. You will learn how you can partner with God so that all of the enemy's attacks can be reversed. And you will also learn how to stand against the enemy's schemes when you have done all to stand.

If you are new to the concept of spiritual warfare, I want to welcome you on this journey. We will have fun learning about our identities and how much power we carry when we partner with Jesus, the author and perfecter of our faith. Spiritual warfare does not have to be difficult or scary. It can be as simple as taking our focus off of the enemy and placing it on God where it belongs.

If spiritual warfare has always felt difficult to you, then I want to encourage you—Jesus's death and resurrection is more than enough. You can renounce the lie that warring in the spirit realm is hard and release that mindset to God. Fearing spiritual warfare is a basic tactic from the enemy to keep you discouraged and enslaved to fear. If you are experiencing this lie, I want to encourage you—God is a deliverer by nature. It is not *if* He will deliver you but *when*. If you are in a difficult season or situation, hand it over to God right now and ask Him to step in and reverse the enemy's attacks. God will use the situation you are in to train you and build you up in the skills on how to war wisely. The Bible says:

> *And we know that God causes everything to work together for the good of those who love God and are called according to his purpose for them. For God knew his people in advance, and he chose them to become like his Son, so that his Son would be the firstborn among many brothers*

and sisters. And having chosen them, he called them to come to him. And having called them, he gave them right standing with himself. And having given them right standing, he gave them his glory. What shall we say about such wonderful things as these? If God is for us, who can ever be against us? (Romans 8:28-31 NLT)

CHAPTER 1

So What Is Spiritual Warfare?

For we are not fighting against flesh-and-blood enemies, but against evil rulers and authorities of the unseen world, against mighty powers in this dark world, and against evil spirits in the heavenly places.
—Ephesians 6:12 NLT

Years ago, I was praying for a woman named Ellen. She had come in for prayer and had an obvious heaviness about her. I was eager to see what the Holy Spirit was going to do in her session. As we sat down and began to pray,

I saw a picture in my mind of Ellen cowering as a child and her father erupting into violent rage. As we prayed, I asked Ellen, "Is there anything you need to forgive your father for?"

Tearing up, Ellen said, "Yes, I need to forgive him for treating me so harshly while I was growing up."

Although Ellen's dad had not ever been physically violent, his vocal outbursts had made her feel unsafe. Going through some painful memories, Ellen confessed, "I never knew growing up whether I was going to get hurt or not."

In our session, Ellen and I broke agreement between herself and her father's painful words. For the past twenty years she had been hearing lies like "you're no good" and "I wish you weren't my daughter." I had Ellen hand these negative verbal mental tapes and playlists to God and ask Him for His truth. As she handed God these painful messages, we asked what the Lord wanted to show her. As Ellen and I prayed, she began to hear God's voice and softly cried.

Leaning close, I asked, "What's the Lord showing you?"

After a few sobs, Ellen said, "God keeps telling me 'I'm proud of you. You have loved others so well.'" Wiping her face, she said, "I just can't believe He's saying this to me! It feels so great!"

As Ellen and I continued to pray, she heard more comforting words from her heavenly Father: "You are My protected and beloved, My princess, and My daughter," and "I will never rage at you." Implementing each of these truths from God, we supplanted the devil's lies one by one until she finally heard the biggest truth of all, "I want you to learn to love yourself the way I love you."

At the end of our session, Ellen asked God to forgive her for all the negative self-talk she had believed and added to her father's words. She broke agreement with self-hatred, performance, perfectionism, and fear of failure. She commanded these ungodly spirits to leave, and when we finally shut all the open doors to the enemy, she literally sank back into her seat as an evil presence left the room.

Immediately, the physical brightness in the room increased as Jesus, the Light of the World, stepped in and dispelled darkness. In a few hours, Ellen had gone from feeling discouraged and tormented to being completely set free and experiencing a greater connection with her heavenly Father.

This is one of the many spiritual encounters I come across daily. As an inner healing and deliverance minister, I meet with people often from various walks of life. It is a true joy to experience God's goodness in our sessions by seeing how He reaches in and handles each person's pain. In all my years of praying for people, I have seen more and more of God's true nature, and it fills me with joy every day. In some way, God's love always comes through and brings radical transformation.

THE ESSENTIALS

For some of us, *spiritual warfare* may sound like a vague term. The phrase may creep up in a sermon or jump out at us from a book, but for many of us spiritual warfare exists as a nebulous subject rarely ever on our minds. However, according to Scripture, being adept at spiritual warfare is extremely important, and as the Bible shows, spiritual warfare is very real.

Again, spiritual warfare is the invisible war between good and evil—the conflict between us, God's children, and satan, the enemy of our souls. Now, before you start to panic about being at war with the devil, remember you are on God's winning team. When we confess Jesus as our personal Lord and Savior, we come under His blood. The devil and his minions no longer have power over us.

When we live in the reality that we are God's, we come under the promise that we are both loved and protected (see John 3:16; Luke 10:19). When we come under the shadow of His wings and walk in this reality, there is nothing the enemy can do to defeat us (see Ps. 91:4).

The challenge to being successful in spiritual warfare is learning how to walk in God's protection, so the enemy's attacks and lies can't harm us. God has given us a shield of faith to extinguish the enemy's fiery darts (those lies or assignments he is trying to throw at us [see Eph. 6:16]). When we partner with the enemy's lies, we give them power and allow the devil unnecessary influence over our lives. If we stay focused on God's truth and refuse to allow the enemy to have a place of influence, we become shielded from his attacks and stand in the authority that we have been given as God's beloved children. Like Jesus, we become experts at sleeping in the midst of our storms:

On that day, when evening had come, he [Jesus] said to them, "Let us go across to the other side." And leaving the crowd, they took him with them in the boat, just as he was. And other boats were with him. And a great windstorm arose, and the waves were breaking into the boat, so that the boat was already filling. But he was in the stern, asleep on the cushion. And they woke him and said to him, "Teacher, do you not care that we are perishing?" (Mark 4:35-38)

If we are truly partnered with Christ, then we should be able to abide in His peace at all times. Living in His peace, we can easily say no to satan when he tries to tempt us to partner with him. The devil can't force us to partner with sin, and like Jesus, we can't be forced to be afraid of the waves. Understanding the great power of the cross is our building block on which we can stand in spiritual warfare. The next time you feel attacked by the enemy, take a step back and ask the Lord what He thinks of your situation. I promise you the more you stay focused on His goodness, the more empowered you will be.

WHERE WE WAR FROM

For a more in-depth explanation on spiritual warfare, let's look at some Scriptures. Many of us have heard sermons on how God gave man authority over the earth, then lost it to satan, and then regained it through the death and resurrection of Christ. In Genesis, Adam and Eve walked in communion with God, but because of the fall, a wall/veil between themselves and the Lord was erected. It wasn't until thousands of years later when Jesus died and was resurrected that the veil was torn so we could once again commune daily with God.

In Genesis, when satan tempted Eve and caused her and Adam to sin, their relationship with God was severed. Man was removed from the garden, and satan was given authority over the earth (the physical realm).

When Jesus died on the cross and was resurrected, He took back the authority man had given to satan. Retaking His seat in Heaven, Jesus gave mankind all of His authority and told us to make disciples of all the earth (see Eph. 1:19-23; Matt. 28:19).

Today the enemy's strategy is to trick us into believing the devil still has the authority. He wants us to believe we are still subjected to his schemes, tricks, and temptations, but that is simply not true. When we are born again, we become seated with Christ in the heavenlies (see Eph. 2:4-6). As we fight from this position, we become wise, unstoppable warriors.

In Second Corinthians, Paul gives us a glimpse of exactly where we should war from. Consider this verse:

> *I know a man in Christ who fourteen years ago—*
> *whether in the body I do not know, or out of the*
> *body I do not know, God knows—such a one was*

caught up to the third heaven (2 Corinthians 12:2 NKJV).

In this verse, Paul reveals there are at least three heavenly realms. Many theologians today divide these categories into the *first heaven,* the *second heaven,* and the *third Heaven.*

The first heaven is categorized as the physical realm around us (what we can see and/or touch with our physical senses—like the sky). The second heaven is the unseen spiritual realm where God's angels and satan's demons do combat. The third Heaven (God's actual dwelling place) is where we are seated with Christ and from where we should be doing our warfare.

When we try to engage our earthly, first heaven realities, we end up fighting the people around us (flesh and blood) instead of the enemy (satan's spiritual forces). Warring from this realm, we strain from the ground to push up against the enemy and his attacks. This positions us beneath the powers of the enemy (since the first heaven is below the second heaven) and prevents us from warring with full effectiveness. Fighting with this mindset, we find ourselves struggling to lift off the weight of the demonic oppression that is targeting us.

When we do warfare in the second heaven, we enter a boxing ring where we fight against the enemy on his own turf. Boxing the demonic at this level, we get in a few good punches, but we also experience our fair share of retaliating shots. When we war in the second heaven, we miss out on our true authority because we are neglecting God's gift of being seated with Him in the third Heaven. Spending too much time squabbling with our foe and failing to connect with the Lord's revelations and strategies, we end up receiving more hits than we give. If we are to be truly effective warriors, then we must do spiritual warfare from God's position of power.

When we engage in spiritual warfare in the second heaven, we fight as opponents—not champions. We position our skills and strengths against the enemy's. This rarely produces a sustaining victory because satan and his forces have had centuries to perfect their skills. It is to our benefit to allow the angelic realm to do the boxing for us as we remain seated with Christ in the third Heaven. A passage showing this type of second heaven warfare can be seen most vividly in Daniel:

> *And behold, a hand touched me and set me trembling on my hands and knees. And he said to me, "O Daniel, man greatly loved, understand the words that I speak to you, and stand upright, for now I have been sent to you." And when he had spoken this word to me, I stood up trembling. Then he said to me, "Fear not, Daniel, for from the first day that you set your heart to understand and humbled yourself before your God* [on earth/ from first heaven]*, your words have been heard* [in heaven/third Heaven]*, and I have come because of your words. The prince of the kingdom of Persia withstood me twenty-one days* [in the second heaven]*, but Michael, one of the chief*

princes, came to help me, for I was left there with the kings of Persia [second heaven], *and came* [appearing physically in the first heaven] *to make you understand what is to happen to your people in the latter days. For the vision is for days yet to come"* (Daniel 10:10-14).

In this passage, an angel described the conflicts happening in the second heaven. Whereas the messenger angel was delayed, Michael, one of God's archangels, was dispatched to bring reinforcements. This allowed the first angel to become disentangled from his second heaven foe and deliver his message to Daniel in the physical realm (the first heaven).

When we engage in spiritual warfare from the third Heaven (our victorious place of rest where we are seated with Christ), we become spectators and allow God's army to do the fighting for us. This is the only position where satan is under our feet. Interestingly, in Scripture it is the God of Peace who crushes satan under our feet (see Rom. 16:20).

MORE THOUGHTS ON WARFARE

Other than Jesus Himself, the apostle Paul is one of the Bible's most prolific thinkers on spiritual warfare. Paul gives us some incredible insights into how this area of battle works. When I travel, the apostle Paul is one of the writers I most often refer to when I am teaching on this subject. Consider this famous passage from Ephesians:

For we are not fighting against flesh-and-blood enemies, but against evil rulers and authorities of the unseen world, against mighty powers in this dark world, and against evil spirits in the heavenly places (Ephesians 6:12 NLT).

Paul's verse shows us our enemies are not flesh and blood (what we physically see around us). Our neighbors, leaders, spouses, and teenage children are not the enemies we should be fighting, nor the political figures or agenda pushers with whom we strongly disagree.

We must learn to take our focus off of what is going on in the physical realm around us (the first heaven) and aim our prayers at what God is doing in the spiritual realm. Jesus encourages us to invest ourselves in what is going on in Heaven rather than on earth because He knows the more we invest in eternity, the more our physical surroundings will reflect that reality. Consider this verse:

Do not lay up for yourselves treasures on earth, where moth and rust destroy and where thieves break in and steal, but lay up for yourselves treasures in heaven, where neither moth nor rust destroys and where thieves do not break in and steal. For where your treasure is, there your heart will be also (Matthew 6:19-21).

Jesus instructs us to pay attention to what is going on in the spiritual realm and even encourages us to put our treasures and values in that area. This solidifies the idea that the spiritual realm at least influences, if not actively engages, with the natural. Jesus, like Paul, encourages us to keep our minds focused on what is going on in the unseen realms. We are not just meant to thrive here on earth physically. We are meant to thrive spiritually as well. Consider this verse:

> *Set your minds on things that are above, not on things that are on earth. For you have died, and your life is hidden with Christ in God* (Colossians 3:2-3).

Unfortunately, most of us tend to focus only on what is going on physically around us, and this is a major tactic of the enemy. When we engage only in the physical realm, we fail to do battle against the unseen forces that are behind the scenes pulling the strings.

In the story of Elisha and his servant, we saw how one man's eyes (Elisha's servant's) were closed to the spiritual realm. When the enemies of God surrounded Elisha, his servant saw only the Persian armies amassing against them. Not feeling any fear, Elisha said, *"Do not be afraid, for those who are with us are more than those who are with them"* (2 Kings 6:16). God opened the eyes of Elisha's servant and allowed him to see the truth that he was surrounded by angels—and not just the physical Persian enemy.

Like Elisha's servant, we need to stop focusing on what is happening around us, and pay attention to what is going on behind the scenes. As the Bible points out, there is an entire spiritual world moving around us. If we acknowledge the spiritual realm and allow the Lord to open our eyes to its influence, then we will see just how protected and equipped for spiritual battle we are.

THE SPIRITUAL REALM IS VERY REAL

Most Christians have trouble relating to the spiritual realm because, obviously, it is difficult to see. However, to be truly effective, we need to take the subject of the spiritual realm seriously. Much of what we see in the physical realm has a spiritual reality behind it. When I see a person acting out in rage, it is most likely not just that person partnering with a bad mood. Quite possibly, there is a literal spirit of rage tormenting that person and he or she is agreeing with it and therefore coming under its influence.

Have you ever heard the phrase, "I just woke up on the wrong side of the bed"? I have news for you—there is no wrong side of the bed! There is just you and God and the spiritual realm. If you are not careful, you will pick up on the unhealthy broadcasts that are being sent out in the spiritual realm and start acting out of them accordingly. Part of a Christian's job is to learn how to discern what is going on around them spiritually so they won't end up partnering with what is in opposition to God.

When we partner with what God is saying and fight from a heavenly perspective, we more easily overcome the enemy's schemes. Just as Jesus calmed the storm with His disciples, we get to rest in God's goodness and renounce any and all attacks the enemy is waging against us. This is the simple reality of spiritual warfare for the redeemed

Christian and is one of the core messages of this book. Be encouraged by Christ's words:

> *Behold, I have given you authority to tread on serpents and scorpions, and over all the power of the enemy, and nothing will injure you* (Luke 10:19 NASB).

CONCLUSION

If you are a Christian, spiritual warfare should not be a heavy burden. As you partner with God and watch His plans become reality, you should feel encouraged. Rather than dreading the enemy's attacks, begin to see spiritual warfare as an opportunity to watch God intervene in your life. If you are feeling intimidated by the enemy, reflect on these verses below. Trust in God and know you are protected by Him. The devil has no power over you unless you allow it. Read these verses and allow them to pour strength into your spirit:

> *The God of Peace will soon crush Satan under your feet* (Romans 16:20).

> *But thanks be to God! He gives us the victory through our Lord Jesus Christ* (1 Corinthians 15:57 NIV).

> *A final word: Be strong in the Lord and in his mighty power. Put on all of God's armor so that you will be able to stand firm against all strategies of the devil. For we are not fighting against*

flesh-and-blood enemies, but against evil rulers and authorities of the unseen world, against mighty powers in this dark world, and against evil spirits in the heavenly places. Therefore, put on every piece of God's armor so you will be able to resist the enemy in the time of evil. **Then after the battle you will still be standing firm** (Ephesians 6:10-13 NLT).

I can do all things through Christ who strengthens me (Philippians 4:13 NKJV).

*But you belong to God, my dear children. You have **already won** a victory over those people, because the Spirit who lives in you is greater than the spirit who lives in the world. Those people belong to this world, so they speak from the world's viewpoint, and the world listens to them. But we belong to God, and those who know God listen to us* (1 John 4:4-6 NLT).

As you begin this journey in growing in your understanding of spiritual warfare, allow these verses to seep in and speak to your heart. Get alone with God, and ask Him how He sees your role in the wider realms of spiritual warfare. Ask Him for a verse for confirmation, and as you go throughout your week, see what truths He provides. I promise, you will not be disappointed. God is talking all the time. All we have to do is open our spiritual ears and listen.

Summary

Points to Ponder

Though an act of war, spiritual warfare can be fought from a place of peace. A perspective shift might be needed to actually see this play out in your life.

Verse to Remember

The God of Peace will soon crush Satan under your feet.
—Romans 16:20

Questions

1. In what ways can I partner with God to bring His presence more clearly into my daily life?

2. Have there been times when I didn't take the spiritual realm seriously?

3. What does Father God want me to know about the spiritual realm?

4. How does God want me to start practicing my awareness of the spiritual realm?

5. What does Father God want me to know about my seated position with Christ?

PRAYER

Thank You, Jesus, for Your sacrifice and for reconciling me with God. Open my spiritual eyes to see what You are doing. As I sit with You in the third Heaven overlooking the enemy's schemes, show me Your perspective of my current situations.

ACTIVATION

Pray over your situation now with the knowledge God has provided you.

CHAPTER 2

HOW WE WAGE WAR

*We use God's mighty weapons, not worldly
weapons, to knock down the strongholds of
human reasoning and to destroy false arguments.
We destroy every proud obstacle that keeps people
from knowing God. We capture their rebellious
thoughts and teach them to obey Christ.*
—2 CORINTHIANS 10:4-5 NLT

*Finally, be strong in the Lord and in the
strength of his might. Put on the whole
armor of God, that you may be able to
stand against the schemes of the devil.*
—EPHESIANS 6:10-11

Years ago, I ran into an angry couple at my bank. They were standing by the main door and were arguing heatedly—although I don't remember exactly what it was about. As their intensity grew, I found myself feeling more and more anxious, and as I made my way past them, I could hear my mind screaming, "This isn't safe! What if they turn violent?"

Walking past, I prayed God would release peace into their situation. Amazingly, as soon as I prayed, the fear left me and I began to feel better. My attitude continued to improve as I made my way to the car.

However, once I reached my car another emotion flooded over me. This time it was rage. I turned back and thought, *How dare those people fight in front of me! Someone could have been hurt.*

Seething with rage, I headed toward the bank's doors, but then thought, "What if this is another atmosphere the enemy is trying to get me to partner with? What if I could shift their atmosphere instead?"

I stepped back into the bank and again walked right past the couple (who were still arguing) and quietly prayed that God would release His peace and remove any traces of fear *and* rage. As soon as I prayed, the angry couple paused and looked up at each other, flustered, and said, "Whatever" and went their separate ways. Because of my willingness to partner with God's prompting, I was able to release His peace into the midst of their situation.

RULES OF WARFARE

The devil may try to enlist the help of other people to attack us, but it is more common for him to try and sneak lies/ungodly thoughts into our minds. Some thoughts, as in the example above, come from external broadcasts the enemy is releasing over a person, place, or region. Other thoughts, as we will examine in this chapter, come in the form of demonic whisperings (I-messages) that aim to tear down our relationships with others, ourselves, and God.

Understanding our "normal" mindsets in day-to-day life will help us tremendously in discerning what is going on around us in the spirit realm. It is up to us to guard our thoughts and become careful stewards of what we think. Over the years, I have found much of our daily battles occur in the mind. If we are not able to take authority over our thoughts, then we will not be able to take authority over the spiritual realm that is trying to influence us.

CONQUERING THE MIND

As Christians, much of our job in spiritual warfare is casting down the negative thoughts and imaginations the devil raises against us and our God. These negative thoughts and imaginations, coming at us in the form of lies, try to obscure the revelation and goodness of God and His character. When we believe the enemy's lies, we come under his falsehoods and live under their influence. When we reject the enemy's lies and ask the Lord for His truth, we sidestep the devil's attacks and walk in our true identity.

23

Lies (ungodly thoughts and imaginations) are the most common attacks the enemy uses against us. This is because lies are so easy to get us to believe when we think they are our own. Simply put, lies are false statements that weaken our connections with God and others. Lies can be as simple as "God doesn't love me" or as complex as "Because of this past sin I committed years ago, God won't come through for me today."

Lies come in all shapes and sizes. They can be subconscious, where they exist at an unknown level, or fiercely overt where you are actively participating with them, like when you choose consciously to believe a lie. No matter how lies manifest themselves in your life, they need to be surrendered to God and replaced with His truth. Otherwise you will continue to keep acting out of their negative design and creating bad fruit in your life.

When learning how to master spiritual warfare, you need to develop the habit of asking God to show you what specific tactics the enemy is using in your situation. More often than not, his attacks will either be through playing on a lie he has earlier implanted in your mind or through a demonic broadcast he is releasing (like in the story about the couple). Once you discern the type of attack the enemy is lobbing against you, you will be able to wield the proper weapons God has for you in battle. By submitting your thoughts to Christ, you learn how to take ownership over the battle in your mind and present yourself as an unstoppable warrior for the Kingdom.

TACTICS OF THE ENEMY

Because the devil is spirit, the weapons he uses against us are spiritual as well. Satan's primary weapon is deception, and part of his goal is getting us to believe the lies he presents about others, ourselves, and/or God. As the "father of lies," satan excels at tempting us with false statements—sowing seeds of suspicion and accusation (John 8:44). Rooting out satan's lies and replacing them with God's truth is a major component of the Sozo ministry I colead with Teresa Liebscher. If a person receiving prayer is able to identify the presence of demonic lies in their life, then they can partner with God to reject their influence and ask the Holy Spirit for His truth.

In Scripture, Paul tells us our primary weapons are "God's mighty weapons" and our job is to "knock down the strongholds of human reasoning" and "false arguments" that are raised against the knowledge of God (2 Cor. 10:4-5 NLT). In essence, we are called to refute every thought, idea, or spirit standing in direct conflict with the Lord. Submitting our thoughts to God becomes a valuable step in keeping our minds above the enemy's attacks.

Cleaning out the garden in our minds is a daily task we must learn if we are to identify bad fruit in our lives. As we replace the bad fruits with truths found in God's Word, we become more and more like our Father in Heaven. Once the devil's lies are pulled out and replaced with God's truth, a healthy, heavenly mindset develops. Scripture says:

Finally, brothers, whatever is true, whatever is honorable, whatever is just, whatever is pure, whatever is lovely, whatever is commendable, if there is any excellence, if there is anything worthy of praise, think about these things (Philippians 4:8).

I-MESSAGES

Perhaps one of the most common forms of lies the devil presents to us are what I call I-messages. These are lies that appear in the first-person voice. They clothe themselves in our own voice to try and trick us into more easily partnering with them. The goal of these lies is to get us to believe them by thinking they are our own thoughts. I-messages can be targeted at others and work at severing our connections with our fellow friends and family members; they can target our own psyche and try to wear down our self-confidence; and they can target our relationship with God and try to sever our connection with Him.

I-messages targeting our relationship with God are perhaps the most dangerous because they seek to keep us separated from God's love. I-messages aimed at others are equally destructive because they work to separate us from the help and affection others can give us. I-messages aimed at others tend to sound like, "I am so glad I am not working with this person anymore. He is such a creep." I-messages targeting ourselves can sound like, "I am so ugly. No one in the world will ever want to marry me." I-messages harming our relationship with God can be thoughts like, "I am such a loser. There is no way God really loves me."

A lot of our success in spiritual warfare begins with us partnering with God to take authority over I-messages. Once we take ownership over these thoughts and submit them to Christ, we will be able to more easily discern them and renounce their influence. Only when we encounter God's truth and implement it into our lives can we truly be set free from them. Scripture says:

> *If you abide in my word, you are truly my disciples, and you will know the truth, and the truth will set you free* (John 8:31-32).

Many of our spiritual battles begin in the mind. This is precisely why Scripture spends so much time teaching us how to steward it. The apostle Paul tells us we are to take captive "every thought" that comes into our minds (2 Cor. 10:5). This does not mean only half of our thoughts or even three-quarters. Instead, we are to take *every* thought captive, for if we cannot master our own thoughts, how can we be expected to resist the enemy around us?

Our job as Christians is to renounce these I-messages and refuse to allow them any place of influence. As we replace the enemy's lies with truth, we expand God's Kingdom and set ourselves up for spiritual success.

. . .

This reminds me of the season when my son was dealing with struggles of suicide. At times over several years, Cory's internal battles in his mind would explode in external outbursts of, "I should just kill myself!" Since this was obviously a terrifying statement for a parent to hear, I would lovingly try to confront him. We would look at the lies he was believing—about failing, not measuring up, and never being good enough—and hand them to Jesus and ask for His truth. As we prayed through these lies, his threatening outbursts became less frequent.

However, it did not completely stop his internal dialogue. While I was in prayer, the Lord revealed to me, "Your son is struggling with depression and suicidal feelings because he is partnering with a catastrophic spirit. If he will break agreement with this spirit, then his struggle with suicidal thoughts will end."

After I broke agreement with my own thoughts of feeling overwhelmed, I took Cory aside and explained to him what God had shown me. This was a loving confrontation that gave him insight into his battles. Once I explained what God had showed me, he repented of partnering with this catastrophic spirit and for partnering with the suicidal thoughts that were becoming a normal way for him to protect himself from feeling stressed and afraid. We both walked away that day with a new measure of freedom, knowing how to choose which thoughts we could entertain and which ones we could reject.

Cory left that moment with the demonic stronghold broken, yet he still needed to keep the door to suicide closed. Later when struggling with being overwhelmed, he'd say, "Jesus, I'm feeling a little worn out right now. Can you please give me some truth so I can make it through this situation?" Once he understood suicide was not a thought originating in his own mind but a devastating lie sneaking in from the enemy, he was able to take it captive and make it obedient to Christ.

MORE ON I-MESSAGES

A lot of our success in spiritual warfare begins with us partnering with God to take authority over our minds. The Holy Spirit, as our teacher and our comforter, guides us in girding ourselves with truth. When we partner with the Holy Spirit, the enemy's lies are revealed. Grounding ourselves in His wisdom and God's Word, we allow the Lord's truth to pierce our hearts and minds and reveal our situations through the lens of God's truth.

To keep it uncomplicated, I follow a simple rule. If a thought or idea leads me further from Jesus, then it is either my flesh or the enemy trying to influence me with a lie. If a thought or idea leads me closer to Jesus, then either it is His Spirit working in me or my flesh being surrendered to Christ.

To help you understand more about I-messages and where such thoughts originate, here is a chart below. Feel free to study each column and add a few of your own:

I-MESSAGE	SPIRITUAL SOURCE
"I am so worn out and exhausted. There is no way I am going to make it through this week."	Discouragement
"There is nothing I can do to ever gain freedom."	Hopelessness
"Everyone is against me."	Self-pity/victim mindset
"I can't stand that he got promoted ahead of me."	Jealousy
"I'm sure watching this risqué movie will be fine. After all, I'm a mature believer."	Lust

Understanding that I-messages may not have originated with you is the first step to rejecting their influence and taking them captive. Sometimes, unfortunately, the I-messages we hear are so deeply rooted in our own beliefs that we are unable to discern they are not our own issues until it is too late. When we believe the I-messages that say "I am ugly" or "I am too exhausted to do anything fun" and accept them as truth, then we can only break free from them once we allow the Holy Spirit to step in and speak His truth.

Other I-messages may be more discernible as the enemy's voice because the thoughts are so out of our character (to how we naturally act or behave). For instance, someone who never struggles with sexual sin but suddenly finds himself inundated with perverted thoughts will more easily understand that he has walked into an atmosphere of perversion. In contrast, those who struggle with perversion on a regular basis will have a harder time understanding that perverted I-messages are not their own when encountering a spirit of sexual sin, because they are so used to struggling with such thoughts on a regular basis.

This is why it is so important to learn how to walk in righteousness. When we follow God's truth and live according to His purposes, sinful urges and I-messages stand out like a sore thumb. We instantly recognize them as demonic attacks because they feel so out of touch with God's character and voice of truth.

The more we stay close to God and His ways, the easier it is for us to tell when the enemy is sneaking thoughts and lies into our hearts. This is why if I'm walking into a crowded room or conference and suddenly feel overwhelming panic, I know it's not me. Because I tend to be excited to preach, a sudden appearance of anxiety tells me it is going on in the room around me. Knowing it is not my panic but rather a broadcast of panic, allows me to reject its voice and keep from coming under it.

TAKING THOUGHTS CAPTIVE

The best way to conquer ungodly thoughts or I-messages is to partner with the Holy Spirit and take thoughts captive. One way you can do this is to simply renounce the enemy's voice. A simple prayer you can use is: "I see you, enemy, and I am not partnering with you. I send you back in

Jesus's name and release [insert God's truth here] into my mind instead."

Commanding the enemy's voice to leave you doesn't have to be complicated. You don't have to go through an hour-long prayer listing every unhealthy thought or emotion you are feeling. You can simply hone in on the root problem and renounce it. You can identify the root of a demonic attack by asking the Holy Spirit, "Holy Spirit, what lie is the enemy trying to bait me with?"

Depending on how the Lord responds, you might identify the enemy's attack as *fear, panic,* or *anxiety.* Or you might identify it as *lust, depression,* or *suicide.* Whatever the Lord reveals to you, renounce its hold and ask Jesus to put His truth in its place. Once you hand the enemy's lies over to God, you can ask the Lord for His truth and release it into your life and the surrounding atmosphere. This is what taking thoughts captive and making them obedient to Christ can look like in your daily life. It is also the first step in shifting atmospheres.

USING YOUR GIFT OF DISCERNMENT

For the most part, I think Christians are more discerning than they give themselves credit. However, I feel much of what we discern ends up being believed as our own junk rather than it coming from the enemy. It is our responsibility and blessing to discern what is going on around us in the atmosphere and in our minds, and knowing these steps can help us to reverse demonic influences.

Unfortunately, most of us are not trained in the gift of discernment so we typically have no idea of what to do once we discern the enemy's attack. Many times we simply give in to whatever feelings the enemy is broadcasting and subconsciously partner with his hold. We fail to discern correctly and end up fighting ourselves instead of the devil. When we think the enemy's negative thoughts are our own, we struggle with an exhaustive inner battle that isn't even our own. We must learn to discern where our thoughts and feelings are coming from, so we can do battle against them effectively.

As I mentioned earlier, you can usually tell where I-messages come from if they are negative or somehow pull you away from God. If a thought or feeling comes from the Lord, it will lead you closer to Him. A thought or impression from God might not always lead you to the easiest path, but it will always lead you into what is right.

What the devil presents to you will lead you further down the road of sin and selfishness. If you find yourself being bombarded by thoughts, take a step back and ask yourself where these thoughts are leading you. If they are not bringing you closer to Jesus, then renounce their hold and ask the Lord for His truth. Remember, many of our thoughts may not be our own.

CONCLUSION

Discerning voices can be tricky. If you are unsure whether you are hearing from yourself, God, or the enemy, spend some time with the Lord and examine where your thoughts are coming from. I have heard some experts say our brains think between 60,000–80,000 thoughts a day. That's an average of 2,500–3,300 thoughts per hour. That is a lot of ideas to cull through!

One way to grow in discernment is to practice it on a daily basis. To improve this gift, start working on it today. When you wake up in the morning, take note of how you feel. Do you wake up joyful and excited? When you go to work, do you feel hopeless, stressed, or anxious?

As you go through your day, pay attention to how your thoughts and feelings change. Does your mind seem over-whelmingly positive or negative in the morning? At the end of your day, do your thoughts or general outlook change? Pay attention to how you think or feel throughout your day, and take notice of when your emotions or mood shift drastically. It will give you a lot of information you can use to discern the enemy's attacks over your life.

For example, say you are experiencing thoughts or feelings of rejection. Or maybe you constantly struggle with depression or discouragement. Whichever negative thoughts or feelings are bothering you, realize it is nothing more than an assignment from the enemy. To remove its influence, simply identify its presence by calling it out. Say, "I see you, [whatever it is you are feeling/struggling with], and I am not partnering with you. I send you back in Jesus's name."

If you feel you have partnered with a negative feeling or thought in any way, ask God to forgive you and exchange it for His truth. Say, "Forgive me, Jesus, for partnering with [whatever negative thought or feeling God has shown you]." Say, "I repent and ask You, Jesus, to remove it from my life."

After you have sent back the thought or emotion that is bothering you, ask, "Jesus, what truth do You want to put in its place?"

Following these steps is a lot like the process I call shifting atmospheres. When you come into a house, building, or region or encounter certain types of people who are carrying negative emotions, you can use these steps to identify demonic attacks and reverse their influence.

For example, you might start your day in the best of moods yet quickly dissolve into discouragement. You may walk into a store and feel fear when you previously felt hope or joy. When you experience such shifts in atmosphere, feeling, or emotion, pay attention. This is most likely your discernment telling you the tone in the spiritual realm is off.

The devil rarely ever comes out and says, "Hi, it's me again. I'm here to deceive you." Instead he uses subtle thoughts and disguises them as I-messages like "Life's too hard," "Jesus doesn't love me," and "Why am I even trying to accomplish this task?" to wear you down with discouragement. When you feel these shifts, it is important to not come under their influence, but to rise above them through repentance and partnership with Christ.

If you feel you need more help in this area, ask a trusted friend or leader to help you. Maybe your spouse would be willing to go through these steps with you to help you train your gift of discernment. Training your gift of discernment is always easier when you have another person to bounce ideas off of. Another set of eyes can be a valuable tool to make sure you are on track. Not all atmospheric shifts need to be drastic. Sometimes they are very subtle. When you identify the atmospheric shifts in your life, renounce them immediately and ask God for what He wants you to release in their place.

SUMMARY

POINT TO PONDER

Not every thought in your head comes from you. Sometimes the devil, your flesh, and even the Lord speaks. God wants you to grow in your ability to discern the voices around you so you can better partner with Him and grow in your skills of spiritual warfare.

VERSE TO REMEMBER

We use God's mighty weapons, not worldly weapons, to knock down the strongholds of human reasoning and to destroy false arguments. We destroy every proud obstacle that keeps people from knowing God. We capture their rebellious thoughts and teach them to obey Christ.
—2 Corinthians 10:4-5 NLT

QUESTIONS TO CONSIDER

1. Have you ever felt powerless in a situation? If so, what did you try to do to make up for it?

2. Do you find yourself having difficulty hearing from the Lord? If so, what steps can you take to increase your spiritual ear?

3. Are there any I-messages that have been plaguing your life? If so, what steps can you take to renounce their hold and replace them with God's truth?

PRAYER

Thank You, Jesus, for speaking to me and giving me tools so I can train my gift of discernment. I renounce all ties with lies and I-messages from the enemy. Help me, Jesus, to stay close to Your truth. Teach me, Jesus, how to renounce the devil's lies so I can stay close to Your perspective. Mold my spirit, soul, and body so they can serve You in Your amazing plan for my life.

ACTIVATION

Ask the Lord for wisdom on how to move through any circumstances with which you are dealing. Ask Him if there are any lies you are believing that are empowering the enemy's hold in your life. If the Lord identifies a lie or I-message, ask Him where you first learned this lie (Was it during childhood? Who taught it to you?). Forgive anyone who taught you this belief, hand it to God, and ask Him what He wants to put in its place. When you receive God's truth, ask Him how you can activate it in a practical way.

CHAPTER 3

WARRING IN BODY, SOUL, AND SPIRIT

*Bless the Lord, O my soul, and forget not all
his benefits, who forgives all your iniquities
[soul], who heals all your diseases [body],
who redeems your life from the pit [spirit].*
—PSALM 103:2-4

Years ago, a woman came in for a Sozo session. She
was in her seventies and had been plagued with physical pain in her joints for almost her entire life. During our
session together, she confessed that in her early twenties

she had had an abortion, which she had never told anyone about until that very moment.

Deciding we should focus on this area, I said, "Repeat after me: Holy Spirit, is there a lie I am believing attached to this secret?"

I sat back and gave her some time to pray. After a few moments of silence, I asked, "Did you hear, see, or sense anything?"

Without hesitation, the woman began to cry. Tears welling, she said, "I feel like God is telling me I never forgave myself for taking the life of my baby. He says I've been holding myself in judgment for so long my body is revolting against me."

Praying together, I had her ask God to forgive her for taking the life of her child. Once she felt God's forgiveness, she forgave herself for making this painful decision. As we walked through these prayers together, she said she felt heat flowing through her body. The woman sat up straight, eyes wide, and said, "Oh my gosh. I can't feel my pain anymore! I think I'm healed!"

SPIRIT, SOUL, OR BODY?

We serve a triune God in whose image we were created, so it should not surprise us we also carry a triune nature. Part of warring wisely is understanding which areas of our beings are under attack so we can use our corresponding biblical weapons to defeat the enemy. Since we are made up of body, soul, and spirit, we may experience an attack in any or all three of these areas. Our body—the physical flesh that ages with us—can be attacked through physical or sexual trauma, fatigue, illness, or by demonic assault. Our souls—our mind, will, and emotions—can be attacked through painful life experiences (trauma), demonic tauntings and/or whisperings, or physical issues that wear down the mind. Our spirits—the part of us that goes to be with Jesus after we die—can be hit with demonic attacks that try to separate us from our connection with God. Learning how to discern each of these attacks and understanding which areas are being assaulted is key in becoming a wise warrior for Christ. In First Thessalonians, Paul writes:

> *Now may the God of Peace himself sanctify you completely, and may your whole spirit and soul and body be kept blameless at the coming of our Lord Jesus Christ* (1 Thessalonians 5:23).

Paul makes a distinction in this verse between our spirit, soul, and body. Once we can discern which types of attacks the enemy is using against us (and which areas of our beings are being attacked), we can use God's weapons provided to us in Scripture to emerge victorious.

I think one reason why there is so much confusion in spiritual warfare today is because there is so much crossover between each of these three areas. For instance, a problem in our body (sickness) can cross over into the spiritual realm (if a demonic spirit is attached and promoting the illness). An issue in the spiritual realm (a broadcast or demonic spirit) might be worsened because of an unhealthy belief system you are entertaining in the mind (soul). Some-times demonic spirits (like a spirit of infirmity) can make you susceptible to physical illness. When we understand which battles we are facing, we can take the proper steps to gain victory.

As we search our hearts and minds to understand from where attacks are originating, the Holy Spirit will walk alongside us and lead us into all truth. James tells us in James 1:5, *"But if any of you lacks wisdom, let him ask of God, who gives to all generously and without reproach, and it will be given to him"* (NASB). Make sure you grow and steward your relationship with the Holy Spirit, for it is from Him that wisdom flows and understanding comes. To help illus-trate the crossovers between body, soul, and spirit, consider this verse:

> *And behold, there was a woman who had had a disabling **spirit** for eighteen years. She was bent over and could not fully straighten herself. When Jesus saw her, he called her over and said to her, "Woman, you are freed from your disabil-ity." And he laid his hands on her, and imme-diately she was made straight, and she glorified God* (Luke 13:11-13).

In this passage, we see the root of this woman's physi-cal torment was spiritually related—being that a disabling spirit (a demon) was crippling her body. Once Jesus delivered the woman from this disabling spirit, healing instantly followed.

MORE CROSSOVERS IN SPIRIT, SOUL, AND BODY

To see more examples on crossovers between body, soul, and spirit, here are some additional verses. Consider this verse from Psalms:

> *Have mercy upon me, O Lord; for I am weak:*
> *O Lord, heal me; for my bones* [body] *are vexed*
> [soul] (Psalm 6:2 KJV).

How is it possible for our bones to be vexed? How can our physical bodies feel emotion? Though David's passage here is poetic, it communicates a bridge between our physical reality (what we are feeling in our bodies) and the emotional realm (what we are experiencing in our thoughts and minds). I have found our physical ailments sometimes carry an emotional/soul attachment. To break free from physical issues that are assaulting us, we may need to take charge and renew our minds. Here is another example from Psalms of this same body and soul crossover:

> *Blessed is the man against whom the Lord counts*
> *no iniquity, and in whose spirit there is no deceit.*
> *For when I kept silent, my bones* [body] *wasted*
> *away through my groaning* [soul] *all day long*
> (Psalm 32:2-3).

In this Psalm, David writes about how when he kept silent about his sin, not only was his soul grieved, but his body was affected as well. We find a reference and an answer to this type of sickness in the New Testament. Here is the passage below:

> *Is anyone among you sick* [physical]? *Let them call the elders of the church to pray over them and anoint them with oil in the name of the Lord* [spiritual]. *And the prayer offered in faith will make the sick person well; the Lord will raise them up. If they have sinned, they will be forgiven* [soul]. *Therefore confess your sins to each other and pray for each other so that you may be healed* [physical] (James 5:14-16 NIV).

In this passage, all three areas of our lives are being addressed. When someone is sick (physical), we are to gather the church together and pray (engage the spiritual realm for healing). If sin is involved, the person can confess his or her sins and be forgiven (the soul) while the Lord breaks any spiritual dynamics that are holding him or her in bondage.

Analyzing this passage, we can see that by confessing our sins, we can close any doors to the enemy and position ourselves for breakthrough. In fact, closing doors to the enemy is a great way we can break the power of sin in our lives and rebuke any harassing, unclean spirits. This is a tool I use often in the Sozo ministry that I call the "Four Doors."

Here is another verse showing the relationship between the soul and flesh realms:

My son, give attention to my words; Incline your ear to my sayings. Do not let them depart from your eyes; Keep them in the midst of your heart [soul]; For they are life to those who find them, And health to all their flesh (Proverbs 4:20-22 NKJV).

As we see in this verse, meditating on the truths of God and implementing His truth into our lives provides health and life to our bodies.

Body, Mind, Spirit Boundaries

When Jessica came in for her Sozo session, I could tell she felt exhausted. Trying not to overwhelm her, I asked calmly, "What's going on?"

Sighing heavily, Jessica said, "Every night around 2:00 a.m. I get woken up by this evil presence. It stands at the foot of my bed and taunts me no matter what I do. Nothing I have tried gets rid of it."

Jessica went on to describe that even when she tried to take thoughts captive, the spirit wouldn't go away. After months of facing this torment, Jessica's body began to wear down and show signs of chronic fatigue.

After telling me her story, I asked Jessica, "Do you mind if we pray for your body?"

"Sure," she said.

I laid my hands on her shoulder and invited the Holy Spirit to bring His peace. Instantly, she began to feel "liquid love" flowing from her head down to her feet. As the Holy Spirit began filling her body, she began to feel exhaustion and burnout leave.

After praying, I asked Jessica if we could tackle the tormenting thoughts and discouragement that were being harbored in her mind. Jessica said yes, and we asked her mind to forgive her for trying to do battle against the demonic without any help from her spirit. When we asked the Lord to strengthen Jessica's spirit and to partner with her in warfare, Jessica relaxed and finally felt a shift toward Heaven's peace. Ending our session together, Jessica sighed and said, "For the first time in months, I don't feel afraid."

At the end of our session, Jessica felt mentally, spiritually, and physically renewed. She even left my office healed from her diagnosis of chronic fatigue.

As Scripture indicates, it is not always easy to discern if what we are experiencing is spiritual, physical, or emotional. Because so much of what we experience intertwines with each other, it can often feel confusing and overwhelming. As you practice listening to the Lord and get better at discerning the origins of the attacks against you, you will be able to more easily navigate the hidden minefields of spiritual warfare. Partnering with Jesus, you will be able to come up with strategies that reverse the enemy's influence.

For example, if you are walking into your place of work and suddenly feel an intense pain in your neck, you will need to discern if this is yours (did you tweak your neck on the way in?) or if it is a word of knowledge (does someone at your job have pain in their neck?) or if there is a spiritual component in the atmosphere you are picking up (are you or others feeling like everyone in the office today is a "pain in the neck"?). Checking in with God as you feel and experience these shifts will give you clarity and insight into your situation. After you take note of your thoughts and feelings, you can work with God to come up with a plan of attack.

After you discern the type of attack being launched against you, you can follow the leading of the Holy Spirit to reverse its influence. In the example above, if you experience sudden pain in your neck that you didn't have moments before and did not injure yourself on the way into work, you can ask, "Holy Spirit, what are You trying to show me?" If the Holy Spirit highlights someone in your office who is rubbing their neck, then He is probably wanting you to step out in faith and pray for their healing (using your spiritual authority to affect the physical realm).

If you picked up the feeling in your neck and you are also feeling irritated, then the Holy Spirit is probably wanting you to renounce a spirit of irritation in the atmosphere. Instead of partnering with irritation, you can renounce its influence and release kindness in its place (this is the basic concept of shifting atmospheres). Or maybe this pain you are experiencing is coming from a coworker who simply brought his own irritation to work. If you have a good relationship with this person, you can kindly ask him what is going on and allow him to process his feelings.

Getting in the habit of being able to discern what is going on around you and using it as information to help you bring God's Kingdom to earth will make you a very effective warrior for Christ. Spiritual warfare does not have to be difficult or scary. Picking up on the enemy's or atmosphere's broadcasts can be easy and fun. Knowing this type of information gives you the insight you often need to pray appropriately.

Now, before we continue, I want to pause for a moment to clarify that although I do believe the spiritual realm is constantly affecting our physical realities, I do not want us to think every single problem we face is caused by demons. Sometimes our bodies are simply telling us it is time to slow down and relax. Pain can be a helpful way for our bodies to tell us to rest, get some sleep, or watch our step.

KNOWING THE BATTLE: SPIRIT, SOUL, OR BODY

When it comes to spiritual warfare, it is important to know our bodies are not equipped to fight off evil spirits. They cannot renounce lies or rebuke ungodly mindsets. And you can't walk into a room and physically punch a demon that is annoying you. Only our souls (our minds) and their partnerships with God can take ownership over our thoughts, and only our spirits, in partnership with God, can take authority over evil spirits.

Our souls (minds) cannot fight off infections or diseases or ward off evil spirits. While improving our lives through positive thinking is possible, having a positive mind does not make diseases go away. Otherwise, getting healed would simply be mind over matter.

Our bodies (God's temples) are at the very least housing units for God's Spirit. As we partner with Him, our bodies can walk in greater health because as we stay connected to His love, supernatural health and a sense of purpose will follow.

Though our spirits are designed to connect with God and warn us about the enemy's attacks, they cannot take authority over our minds or heal our bodies. To protect our bodies, we must eat well, exercise, get rest, and receive prayer when we need physical healing. Although our bodies can't fight off evil spirits, keeping our bodies healthy is one of the best ways we can maintain the temple God has provided for us. Paul writes:

> *Don't you realize that your body is the temple of the Holy Spirit, who lives in you and was given to you by God? You do not belong to yourself, for God bought you with a high price. So you must honor God with your body* (1 Corinthians 6:19-20 NLT).

I am not a health coach, so I won't give in-depth advice on how to take care of your body (though Beni Johnson's book *Healthy & Free* is a great reference for this subject). I do, however, want to share that we need to pay close attention to the needs and designs of our bodies.

CARING FOR YOUR BODY

Years ago, when I was struggling with severe sciatic pain, my physical therapist told me, "Dawna, you're sitting way too much and the muscles in your legs and bottom have atrophied." Since then, I have worked very hard to make sure I am including motion into my daily routine.

It amazes me to see how God has equipped my body to ward off pain when I give it the movement it needs.

The truth is our bodies are made to move and are not designed to be sitting for long periods of time. When our joints fail to get the movement they need, they get stiff and inflamed. I have a doctor friend who uses this phrase often: "Motion is lotion."

Our bodies are also made up of up to 60 percent water. It is therefore important to replenish this life-giving system. We need to make sure we are fueling our bodies with proper nutrients. Believe it or not, sugar is not your body's friend. As one of nature's most addictive substances, it actually does more harm than good.

When Debbie Bailey, a third-year intern and now my friend, came to work for me, one of her first assignments from God was to get me physically healthy. Although she didn't overwhelm me with rules, she gave me great information on how sugar had a detrimental effect on my body, and how the balance and imbalance in my "gut" could either lead to sickness or health. Debbie has traveled with me extensively for the past few years and has helped hundreds of people to restore balance to their guts, and I am grateful for her wisdom.[1]

Although our spirits can fight off demonic attacks that affect our bodies (when we partner with God), I believe one of the best ways we can equip our physical selves for victory is to take time off from our busy schedules and rejuvenate. Sabbath rests are so important for us to connect with God and allow our bodies and minds to refuel. If you are not taking care of your body and resting, then your emotions and spirit may not be healthy either. Consider this verse:

> *Remember the Sabbath day by keeping it holy. Six days you shall labor and do all your work, but the seventh day is a sabbath to the Lord your God. On it you shall not do any work, neither you, nor your son or daughter, nor your male or female servant, nor your animals, nor any foreigner residing in your towns. For in six days the Lord made the heavens and the earth, the sea, and all that is in them, but he rested on the seventh day. Therefore the Lord blessed the Sabbath day and made it holy* (Exodus 20:8-11 NIV).

The Lord takes rest seriously and so should we. Your body is a temple for the Lord. If you are not caring for it, you will be dishonoring the gift of life God has given you. As Christians, we need to be good stewards of our health. Rest, proper food, hydration, and exercise will help our bodies be strong temples for the Holy Spirit. Neglecting our bodies will leave us open to physical attack and keep us from being as powerful as we can be.

CARING FOR YOUR SOUL

Perhaps the best way to care for our souls (mind, will, and emotions) is through reinforcement of God's Word. Wielding the sword of the Spirit allows us to cut through the attacks of the enemy that he wages against us. As we absorb God's truths, His wisdom renews our minds. When the enemy whispers lies to us, God's truth reinforces our ability to fight and break free from the devil's hold. The more we ingrain ourselves with God's Word, the more the lies from the enemy sound false. This is why God calls His Word a lamp to our path and a guide for our feet (see Ps. 119:105). As we ground ourselves in Scripture, our ability to discern the enemy's lies and deal with them quickly grows immensely.

Part of being successful in spiritual warfare is learning how to equip ourselves with both the written Word of God and His rhema (spoken) word. These are the guardrails that help us to walk a straight path and navigate life's crazy turns. Reading the Scriptures daily, meditating on the truths we have read, and taking time to hear from God in prayer strengthens our ability to discern truth, dispel lies, and renew our minds. For example, when we hear lies like "There is no way you will ever be able to accomplish this," we can remind ourselves that the Word of God says, *"I can do all things through Christ who strengthens me"* (Phil. 4:13 NKJV). Never underestimate the power of God's Word. It is truly a weapon we can use to reinforce our being and protect our minds. Without it, we may be unable to discern the attacks from the enemy. Consider this verse:

> *For the word of God is living and active, sharper than any two-edged sword, piercing to the division of soul and of spirit, of joints and of marrow, and discerning the thoughts and intentions of the heart* (Hebrews 4:12).

Prophetic words are also another weapon we can use to feed our souls. When we feel discouraged, we can revisit the words God has spoken over us in our quiet times and reflect on their truths. Rereading the promises God has spoken over us and refocusing our eyes on the goal can be a great way to rejuvenate our strength in the Lord.

One of my favorite prophetic words ever spoken over me was in a prayer meeting several years ago. I was given a word about me being a banner carrier. The word this person told me was, "In the midst of battle, you are a person who plants God's flag so your fellow warriors can see it and rally around it. Your banner becomes a place of hope that reminds people they are not alone in the heat of battle and that God's army is still alive and fighting." When the enemy tells me that what I am doing doesn't really matter, I remind him that I am a banner carrier who brings hope to others who are lost in the midst of battle, and I am partnering with God to rally His troops.

CARING FOR YOUR SPIRIT

Although it is important to take care of our bodies and minds, we also need to learn how to protect our spirits. Some of the best tools I have used for this are prophetic declarations, worship, and speaking in tongues. Each of these tools instantly awakens my spirit and gives me the necessary fuel to keep charging forward.

When we partner with God with tools like worship, prayer, and speaking truths over ourselves, we become more like Christ because we are connecting with His Spirit. Using these weapons, we become wise warriors!

The enemy's number-one tactic against us is fear. He accomplishes this by deceiving us about the nature of God. He makes himself and our situations feel bigger than the Lord's ability to step in and bring deliverance. As a direct line of communication with God, worship, prophetic declarations, and praying in tongues reset our focus from what is going on around us to who God is in our midst. It reminds us that *"the Spirit who lives in* [us] *is greater than the spirit who lives in the world"* and helps us regain our courage when the enemy is looming over us (1 John 4:4 NLT). These tools remind us we are not facing a fight between two equals. Satan has never been equal to God and never will be. He is simply an annoying pest vying for attention.

All throughout Scripture, we are shown the importance of worship, prophetic declarations, and praying in tongues. In some cases, each of these weapons was used as an act of warfare. Although we will explore some of these weapons later in future chapters, realize for now that using each is a great way to engage your spirit. When I find myself in the midst of battle, these are some of the weapons I turn to, and believe me, once our spirits are engaged with God, we can more easily turn the tide of battle.

CONCLUSION

If you are struggling in spiritual warfare, try to discern where your battle is coming from. If your issue is spiritual, then your strategy may be to worship, pray in tongues, dwell on God's promises, or simply command the ungodly spirits to bow in Jesus's name. If what you are experiencing is targeting your flesh, then you will need to pause and take care of whatever issues are going on in your physical body. This might mean taking a few days off from work to rest, changing your diet, or even altering your routine so your body can heal. Or, if the enemy is trying to tempt your flesh and get you to partner with sin, you will need to take a stand and fight whatever fleshly urges are trying to take ahold of you.

In the cases where your battles are mind-related, you will need to take ownership over your thoughts. Pulling on Scripture, prophetic words, and promises from God will reject any ungodly mindsets that are trying to take ahold of your mind and help you replace them with God's truth.

SUMMARY

POINTS TO PONDER

To be successful in spiritual warfare, it is helpful to know which type of war you are in; is it physical, emotional, or spiritual? Many times, we are unsure how to stand in battle because we aren't sure which area of our lives is being targeted.

VERSE TO REMEMBER

Now may the God of Peace himself sanctify you completely, and may your whole spirit and soul and body be kept blameless at the coming of our Lord Jesus Christ.
—1 THESSALONIANS 5:23

QUESTIONS TO CONSIDER

1. Have you been ignoring the needs of your body?

2. Do you need to implement a new plan for exercising, drinking enough water, eating

the proper foods, and resting so your body can cooperate in its own healing?

3. Have you exhausted your mind by over-working it because you did not understand how the spirit realm was involved in the attack against you?

4. Have you ignored your spirit and paid too much attention to the needs of your body?

5. Have you received any prophetic words about the call on your life?

6. Do you have your own personal prayer language?

PRAYER

Thank You, Jesus, that You are protecting my spirit, soul, and body. I ask You for wisdom so that I can withstand all the enemy's attacks. Protect my mind so that I can stay focused on Your truth. Protect my body so that I can serve You as a temple in my daily life. And protect my spirit so that I can connect with You at all times.

ACTIVATION

Ask the Lord to show you which area you are warring wisely in: Is it your body, soul, or spirit? Ask the Lord which areas you need to improve in. Ask Him for a simple starting point so you can begin implementing changes in these areas (do you need to start some new helpful habits or destroy some destructive ones?). Make a chart or list to help you daily activate these new steps in protecting and equipping your body, soul, and spirit for victory.

NOTE

1. "Sick and Tired of Being Sick and Tired?," Bum Biotics, accessed February 1, 2020, https://www .bumbiotics.com/ sick-and-tired-of-being-sick-and-tired/.

CHAPTER 4

OVERCOMING FLESH BATTLES

*For the desires of the flesh are against the Spirit,
and the desires of the Spirit are against the
flesh, for these are opposed to each other, to keep
you from doing the things you want to do.*
—GALATIANS 5:17

Years ago, I had a young man named Joe come in for a Sozo session. Joe was very gregarious and seemed to have a lot of joy in his life, but as we worked through our session together, I quickly discerned he was hiding something he didn't want me to find.

About halfway through our session, I saw a picture of an old homeless woman. She was bent over with unkempt hair and had filthy clothes. As I watched her painfully shuffle along, I noticed one of her stockings was rolled halfway down her leg.

To be honest, I wasn't sure what this picture meant, but because I felt the Holy Spirit was on it, I related the picture to Joe. As I told him about the image, he began to cry.

"I don't want to give it up," Joe said. "But I told God if He exposed my old friend, I'd repent and hand it over."

"Who is your old friend?" I asked.

"Chewing tobacco," he said.

Joe went on to explain he was addicted to it and had been arguing with God for years about giving it up. He was still reluctant to quit, but then I asked God to show him the desire that his "old friend" (chewing tobacco) had for him. Immediately, Joe sat back in his chair and screamed, "I forsake my old friend now in Jesus's name!"

Surprised at how violent his reaction was, I asked Joe why he was so eager now to break agreement with his old friend. Looking up in horror, he said, "The Holy Spirit showed me a picture of my old friend pulling back my lip. Underneath it was a glob of lip cancer that had eaten away my flesh. It was awful!"

I was not surprised to hear that years later Joe was still tobacco-free.

Much of becoming a wise warrior for Christ depends on our ability to discern what types of attacks the enemy is using against us. Once we learn how to identify the types of attacks he is using, we can partner with Christ to reverse their influence and instill His truth. As we grow in spiritual warfare, it is important to realize that not every battle we face is spiritual. Sometimes our battles are flesh and/or soul related—meaning that they target our minds or fleshly, physical desires.

When discussing the idea of soul versus flesh battles, I typically divide the areas into two categories—*soul wounds* and *fleshly desires*. For the purpose of this chapter, we will focus on fleshly desires and on the battles that specifically target our flesh.

In *Devils, Demons, and Deliverance,* Christian author Marilyn Hickey states that we can figure out whether we're dealing with a flesh or soul issue by understanding this truth: soul issues show up in how we react; flesh issues by how we act.[1]

Flesh issues occur when we battle our desires—those urges that keep telling us "I've gotta have it! I gotta have it!" They tend to lead us to unhealthy or ungodly pursuits. Winning these types of battles sometimes only occurs when we are willing to say no to the temptations and yes to Christ. Consider this verse:

> *No temptation has overtaken you that is not common to man. God is faithful, and he will not let you be tempted beyond your ability, but*

with the temptation he will also provide the
way of escape, that you may be able to endure it
(1 Corinthians 10:13).

Thankfully, God has given us plenty of weapons we can use when fighting against our flesh. Some of these weapons include: 1) taking thoughts captive, 2) clothing ourselves with obedience, and 3) leaning into the Holy Spirit for His strength. When battling the flesh, it might seem impossible to win and stop sinning. However, the Bible says, *"I can do all things through Christ who strengthens me"* (Phil. 4:13 NKJV).

TAKING THOUGHTS CAPTIVE

Scripture commands us to stand when we have done all to stand (see Eph. 6:13). Taking control of our thoughts is one of the best ways we can "stand" when we are facing fleshly desires. Although this is an area we will explore more in the next chapter, it is important here to realize our fleshly actions are very often a direct result of our thoughts. Part of taking thoughts captive is realizing we are not victims to our appetites; we have a choice and a responsibility to say no when necessary.

Our honesty and willingness to follow Christ in all circumstances becomes a powerful act of warfare as we take authority over the thoughts in our mind and choose righteousness—no matter how bad our physical or mental urges feel.

Sy Rogers, an evangelist and international speaker, has a profound testimony in this regard. He lived as a woman for a year and a half when he met Jesus, who changed his life forever. In an article, he wrote:

> To be pleasing to God, to be loved and not rejected by Him—that was all I wanted. As I prayed my life into His hands, trusting Him, the "old man" died and the "new me" was born! What had happened to me? I wasn't sure, but I felt good. Peaceful. Clean. Forgiven. And confident that God would be with me now to help me begin living a decidedly different life.[2]

Although Rogers had a radical conversion and was determined to follow Jesus wholeheartedly, his attraction to other men did not immediately leave. He still had to fight his fleshly desires and walk his deliverance out. Perhaps his internal dialogue became, "I want this [insert name of sin here], but I want Jesus more." Through obedience, Rogers chose his relationship with Jesus over the urges of his flesh and eventually broke the power of its hold over him.

Many times with God, our salvation brings about instantaneous deliverance. We immediately break free from our fleshly desires and rejoice in our newfound freedom. These are some of the most wonderful times. In my own life when I accepted Christ, many of my fleshly urges disappeared and never returned. However, other issues, although disempowered from my life, required me to take action and fight so I could stay free.

In these moments, I had to learn how to walk out my freedom and take hold of righteousness, even on days when I didn't feel like it. Sometimes warring against my flesh became a constant, daily battle as I refused to listen to the whispers of the enemy and turned to the Lord. Eventually, this battle was overcome, but it was not because God appeared and instantly delivered me from my evil desires. This battle was won by me standing and denying my flesh—even when I didn't want to.

I want to encourage you that as you walk in righteousness before the Lord, sometimes you will have to get down in the dirt and wrestle your flesh until you pin it to the ground.

CLOTHING OURSELVES IN OBEDIENCE

Years ago, I was talking to my good friend Renee at our church's coffee shop. While we were ordering drinks, Renee looked at me and said, "Dawna, are you alright? You don't look like you're getting much sleep."

Brushing it off, I said, "I know, but it's fine. I'm not getting a lot of sleep, but boy, am I having fun dreams."

"What kind of dreams?" She asked.

"Well," I started out excitedly, "last night I was having dreams about flying around as a superhero. I was rescuing kids from bad guys. It was so fun."

As soon as I finished, Renee looked at me with concern and said, "Dawna, that is a spirit of fantasy."

Upon hearing her statement, I was dumbfounded. All my life I had loved this aspect of my life. It was so fun to be able to go to bed at night and enjoy my internal "movies." But once Renee had called out my sin, I knew she was right.

God began right there at our coffee shop to show me how I had partnered with this spirit of fantasy since I was a little girl.

When I was young, I would go to bed thinking about how I was exploring new galaxies with Captain Kirk and his Star Trek crew. I would lay my head on my pillow and instantly be transported to a new world of fun and adventure. As I grew, these dreams became romanticized—even to the point of turning into sexual liaisons. Obviously, when I became a Christian, I would edit out these events as they arrived. So, without understanding, as a believer I had religiously continued partnering with this spirit of fantasy. And I was so deceived I didn't even know it.

Now, before you all panic, I do want to point out there is a distinction between God dreams and fantasy dreams. One distinction that showed me I was partnering with fantasy dreams was that upon waking, while I was still excited, I felt tired and worn out. Also, throughout the night, I was able to manipulate my dreams to edit out what I felt was either inappropriate or not as exciting as I liked. With God dreams, you are not able to change what you are seeing, and you should wake up feeling rested.

While I do think imagination is important for creativity, my practice had slid me into a realm of unhealthy fantasy. Instead of getting my fuel and assignments from God, I was getting them from an unhealthy imagination. I was allowing my dream life to be my comfort instead of my relationship with God.

After Renee confronted me on my dreams, I realized how deceived I actually was. I quickly repented before God and said, "I am so sorry for partnering with the spirit of fantasy. Please forgive me and close this door to sin. I give You not only my waking hours but my night life as well."

When I asked God to forgive me and break any agreements I had made with the spiritual realm, God instantly removed the demonic influence that had been controlling my life. He delivered me right then and there, and I knew I had been set free. However, I still had to deny my fleshly desires that kept trying to lead me back into sin. Why? Because later that night, I realized I missed my nighttime friend. My inner nightlife had been meeting a need of significance that wasn't being met now that I had been set free.

When you have been meeting your needs through a partnership with sin, your spirit will need to be delivered from any demonic agreements you have knowingly or unknowingly made. Your flesh may also need to be cleansed if you have opened a door to sexual sin, physical harm, or addiction. Repentance is a mighty weapon you can use as your first line of defense to stand up against these desires.

When fighting a habitual sin, I have found obedience is my greatest weapon.

At first, when I was struggling to resist this former nighttime pattern, I would lay awake feeling myself starting to slip away down the old familiar path. When I felt this start to happen, I would literally say out loud, "I am a child of obedience and I will not partner with you." This was me pulling on the wisdom in Ephesians 6:13 and standing when I had done all to stand.

As I withstood this spirit, its voice became increasingly weaker, and my ability to hear the Holy Spirit grew stronger. I have to say, however, this fight was not easy. At times during the night, I would literally have tears running down my face as I spoke out against the enemy's voice. I had grown so accustomed to balancing out my mediocre days with this fantastical escape that on days when I felt short of other people's expectations, I would feel the desire to slip into fantasy and go away to my happy place where not only was I loved but celebrated.

Eventually, as I continued to wield the weapon of obedience, the fight became easier and the enemy's lure less appealing. Since winning this battle, I have been able to have wonderful dreams with the Holy Spirit—dreams that encourage me and fill me with hope. When I wake up now, I find myself relaxed and fully refreshed.

Although I have never had an alcohol, drug, or sexual addiction, I do know what an addiction feels like—and my addiction was this former escape. It was the pull toward what felt like freedom from life's scary impossibilities. But after my victory, I know now it is possible to stand when you have done all to stand!

The truth is you are not a slave to your fleshly desires. You have overcome by the blood of the Lamb and all your sin has been forgiven by the cross (see 1 John 1:9). Jesus paid for them once and for all. When you asked Jesus into your heart, He made you new (see 2 Cor. 5:17). Do not ever let the enemy deceive you and make you think you can't break free. You can do all things through Christ who strengthens you (see Phil. 4:13).

If you are in a battle against your flesh, confess your sin to God and ask Him to forgive you. Hand Him your unhealthy desires and ask Him to override your urges with His presence in your life. If you need to, tell a friend about the issues you have renounced and ask him or her to hold you accountable in wielding your weapon of obedience.

BOUNDARIES

Another strategy for winning fleshly desires is to set up boundaries consistent with your level of freedom. My husband has a brilliant sermon called "What My Pastor Never Told Me." In it, he makes a distinction between liberty and freedom. Stephen says freedom is an escape from a person, place, or issue, whereas liberty is the capacity to stay free once you have broken through.[3] Webster's dictionary states that freedom is "the quality or state of being exempt or released usually from something onerous."[4]

The Bible says, *"It is for freedom that Christ has set us free"* (Gal. 5:1 NIV). Christ sets us free from a life of sin and death, but He doesn't take away our free will. (See Romans 6:22.)

Webster's dictionary defines liberty as "the power to do as one pleases...the power of choice."[5] My husband likens liberty in Christ as the ability to choose appropriately once set free. In his teaching, he states that freedom without liberty always returns us to bondage. In all my years I have found this to be absolutely true. Many people get free from sin but reopen old doors because they fail to choose righteousness in their daily situations. They fall victim to their old sins because they fail to use their freedom judiciously and protect themselves with healthy boundaries.

Boundaries are a great tool we can use to help us manage our newly found freedoms—especially when dealing with difficult issues such as addiction. Boundaries, in my opinion, help reinforce my character with strength until my choice to not sin becomes my new default.

Each of us should have distinct boundaries that match our level of liberty. My setting a boundary for you may not work. It might feel too loose or too restrictive. You will need to ask the Holy Spirit to give you your own strategies for setting and maintaining boundaries, so you can walk in the measure of liberty that you can manage successfully. I have known men who have been set free from pornography who have had to set extremely strict boundaries for themselves (such as no computers in the home until the lure to pull up pornography is completely mastered).

With regards to my own personal story, I still cannot read romance novels—even Christian ones. For me, it opens a door to the wooing of the fantasy spirit, and it says to me, "Wouldn't it be great to have this type of rescue?" It is also not good for me to watch overly romantic movies.

In our quests to stay healthy, it is important that we become aware of the enemy's schemes to try to reestablish his hold on our lives and set up healthy boundaries accordingly.

LEANING INTO THE HOLY SPIRIT FOR HIS STRENGTH

The enemy's number-one goal in warfare against us is to make us feel powerless. But if we stand fast in our knowledge of God and realize that no temptation is beyond what we can bear, then we will be able to stand firm and resist those fleshly temptations that come from the enemy.

Many times when we are struggling with our flesh, we can come under the lie that tells us it is impossible to overcome. But here are some truths we can use to emerge victorious—when we received Christ, He changed our trajectories. We turned from living in a place of self-satisfaction to living for Him. We left a life of powerlessness and took our rightful place in authority over the enemy and sin. Jesus knows how hard the fight is. He lived as a man but did not sin (see Heb. 4:15). We can rest assured in the goodness of His love and pull on His mercy whenever we need.

It is important to understand that God has made all things new (see Isa. 43:19; 2 Cor 5:17). This includes our ability to withstand our prior propensities to sin. It is an aspect of the immeasurable power of grace—a grace Christ paid for so that we could walk in freedom.

When fighting against the desires of our flesh, we need to lean into the truth of God's Word, follow His Holy Spirit, and apply Christ's blood to our lives. In every circumstance, we need to remember that we are not fighting alone. God sent His Holy Spirit to be our helper, so we can lean into Him and call upon His name whenever we need Him (see John 16:7). God's Spirit will stand with us in our battles to overcome the flesh.

CONCLUSION

Our battles against the flesh might seem impossible to overcome, but don't let this lie overtake you. Through partnership with the Holy Spirit, careful obedience to God's Word, and taking ownership over your thoughts, you can reject the demonic whisperings of the enemy and take authority over your flesh.

Looking at your own life, ask the Lord if there is an area pulling you in the direction of sin. When dealing with fleshly desires, learn how to stand when you have done all to stand. You are not a victim of your flesh. Your desires will bow as you continue to deny the enemy's voice. Get into God's Word, pray, make declarations, erect proper boundaries, be honest with God, and take up your weapon of obedience.

SUMMARY

POINTS TO PONDER

Freedom from sin does not always mean you will never have to battle fleshly desires. Sometimes after being set free, you will need to take authority over the desires of your flesh. You can break free from sinful patterns and conform to the image of Christ as you move deeper into His righteous calling.

VERSE TO REMEMBER

*I can do all things through Christ
who strengthens me.*
—PHILIPPIANS 4:13 NKJV

QUESTIONS TO CONSIDER:

1. Have you ever felt powerless to overcome your flesh?

2. Have you received deliverance in a specific area but have struggled to stay free?

3. In which areas of your life have you won the battle over your flesh?

4. What boundaries have you created in your life to protect your level of freedom?

PRAYER

Thank You, Jesus, for delivering me from the desires of my flesh. I ask that You protect me and keep my mind and body safe. Keep me in Your will so that my life will raise up a sweet and pleasing aroma to You. Thank You for setting me free from the sins of my past. Keep me in the shadow of Your wings.

ACTIVATION

Repent for any areas of sin in your life and break agreement with any demonic strongholds you have partnered with. Command these strongholds to bow in Jesus's name. Repent for any doors to sin you have reopened in your life. Ask the Holy Spirit to clothe you with the mighty weapon of obedience and to show you any new boundaries you may need to implement while establishing proper liberty to match your freedom.

NOTES

1. Marilyn Hickey, *Devils, Demons, and Deliverance* (Dallas: Marilyn Hickey Ministries, 1994), 200.

2. Sy Rogers, "The Man in the Mirror," Exodus Global Alliance, accessed February 4, 2020, https://www .exodusglobalalliance.org/themaninthemirrorp338.php.

3. Stephen De Silva, "What My Pastor Never Told Me," recorded at Bethel Church, 2015, compact disc.

4. *Merriam-Webster*, s.v. "freedom," accessed February 4, 2020, https://www.merriam-webster.com/dictionary/freedom.

5. *Merriam-Webster*, s.v. "liberty," accessed February 4, 2020, https://www.merriam-webster.com/dictionary/liberty.

CHAPTER 5

OVERCOMING SOUL BATTLES

A good tree can't produce bad fruit, and
a bad tree can't produce good fruit.
—Matthew 7:18 NLT

Several years ago, a man named Jeff came in for a Sozo. He was a pastor who had been struggling with an intense addiction to pornography for the last forty years. Although he was Spirit-filled and a great Bible teacher, no matter how hard he tried to stop, he continued to fall back into this sin.

Feeling hopeless, Jeff confessed, "I'm giving God one more chance to set me free. If He doesn't, then I'm finished with Him."

Sitting in my office together, we began to pray. As we partnered with the Holy Spirit, we quickly discovered Jeff's battle with pornography wasn't just a flesh issue. There was a soul wound that needed to be revealed, uprooted, and replaced with God's truth. By the end of our session together, Jeff was feeling relaxed and hopeful. Almost bouncing in his seat, Jeff confessed, "It's finally going to be a fair fight!"

As we saw in the previous chapter, flesh issues are battles that target your flesh. Soul wounds are unhealthy thoughts or mind patterns that cause you to react out *from the flesh*. As author Marilyn Hickey writes, "A problem with your flesh nature will show in how you *act*; a wounded soul manifests itself in how you *react*."[1]

Whenever I teach on the difference between soul and flesh battles, I jokingly use my love of french fries. For example, if I am out to lunch and simply want to eat fries, then this is a flesh issue (a desire). Depending on my resolve, I will either give into this fleshy craving or deny its carnal, unhealthy urge. Soul wounds are different in that they come out of a reaction to a comment made or action taken toward us.

For instance, if I am not craving french fries and someone says to me, "Wow, you have really gained weight," and this interaction makes me want to turn to fries as a source of comfort, then I am reacting out of a soul wound of rejection or hopelessness to lose weight. When I react to comments and situations by choosing sin, it is evidence of a soul issue that needs to be uprooted and healed, rather than a flesh issue that needs to be denied.

Again, flesh issues are evident in how we act when we are not disciplining our bodies. Soul wounds are how we react when a person or situation hurts us. Soul wounds usually involve a deep-seated emotional component that triggers a need in us for self-comfort. French fries, in my case, are simply the physical properties I can turn to in order to get a soul wound of comfort met.

This distinction is important because the weapons we use for battling the flesh are not the same weapons we use when battling issues of the soul. Ephesians 6:13 tells us that when we have done all to stand, stand. This can seem impossible when we are stuck in the midst of battle, but thankfully God has given us weapons we can use in every situation so we can be victorious.

BATTLING SOUL WOUNDS

I used to have a terrible problem with rage. Whenever I found myself in a situation that made me feel overwhelmed, I'd turn and hit the big red button called anger, and it'd make me feel powerful. Obviously, this caused many messes in my home and at work, but in the moments where I felt overwhelmed, rage made me feel as though I had some sense of control. My kids would jokingly call me Nanoo Mom while they were growing up (a nickname they had given me signifying an angry mom species from planet Nanoo).

As I began seeing the destructive power of rage, I started searching God's Word for His perspective on anger. I spent more time with Jesus in prayer and asked Him to help me break free from this cycle. I was surprised to find out, however, how difficult this battle would be.

I clothed myself in God's peace and reminded myself every day that a fruit of the Spirit was self-control. I conformed to Christ's image and watched as rage grew less and less abundant. However, whenever a really stressful situation came up, I'd explode and respond even worse than before. I became so discouraged and felt I would never break free.

When it comes to battling soul wounds (unhealthy thought patterns, lies, and reactions), it may not be enough to simply want to break free. We need to be brave enough and willing to allow the Holy Spirit to reach in and pull out all the deep-seated belief systems that are causing our ungodly responses. Soul wounds stem from lies that target ourselves, others, and/or God. They can be as simple as thinking "God doesn't love me because of my past sin" or as complex as believing "God hates me because of the sin my parents committed generations ago." No matter how simple or complex a lie or belief system may be, they all need to be uprooted. Every lie, ungodly truth, or false mindset is from the enemy. Partnering with any of these falsehoods only leads us down the path to destruction.

No matter what lies or soul wounds are present in our lives, we must hand them over to God and replace them with His truth. The best weapons we can use for this are 1) spending time in God's Word, 2) praying daily and seeking His face, and even 3) attending inner healing and deliverance sessions when needed.

SPENDING TIME IN GOD'S WORD

Because God's Word is so transformational, we can use it like a mirror. As we delve into its truths, we can see how our lives are not conforming to the image of Christ. Studying God's truth, we can allow the Holy Spirit to point out any destructive thought processes that are wearing us down.

For example, if we are feeling fearful but we see in Scripture that Christ was never afraid, we can see that what is in us (being afraid) does not look like Christ. When we read Jeremiah 29:11, *"I know the plans I have for you, declares the Lord, plans…to give you a future and a hope,"* and our thoughts say, "Plans? What plans? I don't really even know that God sees me…" then we know that we have a soul wound of mistrust that we need to heal.

It is important we allow God's Word to penetrate our inner belief systems. I like to tell people to read the Bible out loud and allow themselves to honestly evaluate if what they are reading is creating a positive change in their lives. If not, then there is either a denial of honest evaluation in their own life or there are soul wounds sabotaging their growth. As the source of all truth, God's Word is a piercing sword that can be used to dig out any unhealthy thoughts or lies we are believing. As we get rid of the lies and heal the soul wounds that have been festering in our hearts, the events that previously "triggered" our unhealthy reactions won't hold any power over us.

PRAYING DAILY AND SEEKING HIS FACE

Once a lie or soul wound has been exposed, we need to do some digging with the Holy Spirit and ask Him why we have been believing this lie in the first place. We might even need to ask Him where we first learned this lie and forgive whoever taught us to believe it (like a parent, a friend, or a minister).

For example, in my own life, I learned somehow that I was never good enough unless I outperformed everyone else. When I did my own Sozo sessions, I found that I learned this from my parents. My parents obviously never intended to communicate this lie to me, but internally I always felt pressured to be the best in order to gain their acceptance. Once I confronted this lie and renounced it for God's truth that I was accepted, I was able to forgive my family for making me feel inadequate and ask the Lord to show me how He truly saw me. It has been many years since and I am still free—confident in the love God has shown me.

As we learn to partner with the Holy Spirit and find out why our soul wounds exist, we can work with God to dispel their influence and implement His truth. This is one of the main practices we use in Sozo, the inner healing and deliverance ministry at Bethel Church. By discovering the issues people are dealing with, we can invite the Holy Spirit to come in and gently bring healing.

Using Inner Healing and Deliverance Tools

Sometimes because of fear, shame, or rejection, we do our best to hide our ugly soul wounds and beliefs. We try to cover up any unfavorable reactions so that we aren't judged by our friends, church leaders, and/or family members. Rather than identifying our unhealthy beliefs and surrendering them to Christ, we push our soul wounds further down until they eventually explode and cause a mess. Obviously, this is not the healthy way to live.

The Bible says we are to identify our problems and deal with them head-on, not allow them to fester in darkness. Scripture says:

> *But if we confess our sins to him, he is faithful and just to forgive us our sins and to cleanse us from all wickedness* (1 John 1:9 NLT).

The Bible models that as we confess our sins and the issues troubling our souls, God will step in (forgive us) and bring deliverance (cleanse us from all wickedness). It is time for the Church to stop pretending we are all fine and start dealing with the undercurrent of lies that is producing bad fruit in our lives.

For example, in my own life, my moments of rage became a sign (a warning) of the negative fruit that was growing in my life. Once I was able to step back and see the impact of this fruit, I was able to surrender it to Jesus and get His perspective on my situation. Because I was willing to confront my unhealthy behaviors (and I was not trying to hide them), I was able to get my soul wounds healed and step into the Lord's breakthrough.

ANALYZING OUR FRUIT

A good tree can't produce bad fruit, and a bad tree can't produce good fruit. So every tree that does not produce good fruit is chopped down and thrown into the fire. Yes, just as you can identify a tree by its fruit, so you can identify people by their actions (Matthew 7:18-20 NLT).

This is an undeniable principle found in God's Word. If you have any bad fruit (bitterness, anger, fear, sexual sin) in your life, then it is coming from a bad tree inside of you. This may seem terrifying at first to comprehend, but I have come to love how brain science shows us how the negative thoughts in our minds can bring about negative actions.

What I have come to understand through authors such as Dr. Caroline Leaf (like in her book *Switch On Your Brain*) is that our thoughts (when we first have them) are planted as seeds in the soil of our brains. As life experiences agree with this thought, the seeds become stronger and more rigid. Eventually, when doctors take brain pictures of these fully formed mindsets, they look exactly like trees!

So Jesus wasn't just telling us, "Hey look at that tree over there. Check out its fruit. Cut it down if it's bad." He was telling us to look at the fruit of the mindsets we have.

In our own lives, we must learn to evaluate the fruit that comes from our beliefs and remove all harmful, ungodly mindsets that are producing bad fruit.

This is exactly what happened in my session where I worked with Jeff, the pastor who was trapped in a cycle of pornography. After he and I identified his negative fruit (pornography), we were able to ask God to show us what soul wound was keeping it in place.

Beginning our session, I prayed, "God, would you please show Jeff a memory where he first opened a door to sexual sin?"

Instantly, God took Jeff to a memory when he was fourteen. In the memory, he was carrying fifty-pound sacks of feed. Jesus appeared and showed him how He had helped him carry the sacks of feed all those years ago.

As this memory played out, Jeff began to weep.

"What's God showing you?" I asked.

"God is showing me that it was during this season that I believed I was alone. Later that year, I found pornography in the barn, and when I felt too little for the job, pornography made me feel like a man."

Although Jeff had already been able to identify his bad fruit (pornography), until this moment, he had not been able to confront the soul wound that was keeping it in place ("I am too little for the job"). As we finished our prayer of forgiving his father for abandoning him through death and leaving him as a boy to take over the man's job on the farm, he was able to forsake the mindset he carried into adulthood that he needed to find an alternate way to feel big enough for the task at hand.

Because Jeff's struggle with pornography was not based solely in his flesh, it was almost impossible for him to defeat this cycle until the bad tree (mindset) that produced the bad fruit was revealed, forsaken, and replaced with God's truth. His addiction to pornography wasn't simply a flesh wound; it was anchored in a soul wound/belief system that told him he was alone trying to do a man's job. Whenever someone in church leadership questioned him or doubted a decision, Jeff would spiral back to the memory of being a scared fourteen-year-old boy, and pornography would be there waiting to rescue him.

Yes, Jeff was able in some moments to fight his fleshy desires, but overall his fight was unevenly matched because a soul wound was giving power to his sin. In the midst of doing all to stand, he would eventually give in to his need for self-comfort because of his inner belief system. Today Jeff is completely porn-free and continues to lead in his church. Because of God's grace, the soul wound keeping his sin empowered was destroyed. Finally, it was a fair fight.

CONCLUSION

In my experience, most believers are afraid to deal with the ugly issues that exist in their lives. They instead try to hide their bad fruit. But freedom over our sins and issues is exactly what the Christian life is all about. Since Jesus, our Lord, is perfect, we too must be perfect. Consider this verse:

> *And if you greet only your brothers, what more are you doing than others? Do not even the Gentiles do the same? You therefore must be perfect, as your heavenly Father is perfect* (Matthew 5:47-48).

When we find inappropriate behaviors (bad fruit) leaking out of our lives, we need to partner with God to dispel their influence. Remember that Jesus said we cannot get bad fruit from a good tree. If we have bad fruit in our lives (like in the form of bad behaviors or open sin), we need to ask God why they are there and uproot their influence.

Perhaps the best way to discover the bad fruit in our lives is to pray to the Holy Spirit and ask Him, "Holy Spirit, is there any bad fruit in my life? Are there any lies or soul wounds I need to get rid of?"

Once the Holy Spirit shows us the lies or soul wounds that are affecting us, we can walk through forgiveness and release anyone who may have taught us to view these lies/ soul wounds as truth. The person we might need to forgive for believing these lies might even be ourselves. No matter who the Lord shows us to forgive, we must follow through. Prayers of forgiveness do not have to be complicated. They can be as simple as "I forgive [insert name of whoever God shows you to forgive] for teaching me this lie. I release you from any bitterness in Jesus's name. Amen. Jesus, what truth would You like me to know?"

Once God shows us His truth, we can implement it into our daily lives. This could look like us seizing onto a new mindset and "watering it" with God's Word or implementing a new change in our habits or lifestyle. Whatever truth the Lord reveals, we must be willing to put it into practice on a daily basis so that we can begin to grow godly mindsets instead of ungodly ones.

SUMMARY

POINTS TO PONDER

There is a distinction to be made between battling fleshly desires and soul wounds. Discerning which one of these you are dealing with is the first step toward victory. Be diligent to evaluate the fruit on your tree.

VERSE TO REMEMBER

A good tree can't produce bad fruit, and
a bad tree can't produce good fruit.
—Matthew 7:18 NLT

QUESTIONS TO CONSIDER:

1. Have you received deliverance in a specific area, but your responses to others have not changed?

2. Do you see unhealthy fruit coming out of your life as a response to unfavorable conflicts or situations?

3. When you read the Word, are there verses that you find yourself struggling to identify with?

PRAYER

Thank You, Jesus, for fortifying my soul with Your truth. I ask that You remove any unhealthy soul wounds that have been wreaking havoc in my life. Do Your gentle surgery and replace any lies with Your truth. Forgive me, Jesus, for partnering with soul wounds in the past, and transplant me into a new way of life.

ACTIVATION

Ask the Holy Spirit to show you any bad fruit that has popped up in your life recently, and ask Him to show you why you responded in destructive ways. Allow the Holy Spirit to speak His truth over your situation. Repent for any ungodly responses you have had and break agreement with the lies you have believed. Forgive anyone, including yourself, that has caused you to act negatively. Partner with the Holy Spirit to ferret out the soul wounds in your life and watch as the bad fruit in your life gets replaced with godly fruit.

NOTE

1. Hickey, *Devils, Demons, and Deliverance*, 200.

CHAPTER 6

OVERCOMING SPIRITUAL BATTLES

Pray at all times in the Spirit with every
prayer and request, and stay alert with all
perseverance and intercession for all the saints.
—EPHESIANS 6:18 CSB

Several years ago, I was working late in my office. Everyone had gone home hours before, and as I sat there working, I had this sensation that someone was watching me. I turned slowly and looked outside to see if anyone was there, but to my relief, no one was.

I gathered up my belongings, turned off the lights, and exited the main doors to head home. But as I walked out to the parking lot and toward my car, I still couldn't shake this feeling that I was being watched.

"This is so irrational!" I thought. "What's going on?"

On my way to the car, I found myself turning up the collar on my shirt as if to protect myself from a vampire bite.

"What are you doing, Dawna?" my mind said. "This is so irrational! Vampires aren't real!"

The next day I met with our building's security advisor. I told him about my strange night, and he asked, "Wait, Dawna, what time was that?"

"Seven o' clock," I said.

"Seven?" he said. "That was the same time I was having a panic attack in my bedroom. The whole time I kept saying to myself, 'This is so irrational!'"

It is so important we remember to not only conquer our fleshly desires and heal our soul wounds, but to also do battle well in the spiritual realm. Prayer and worship are powerful tools we can use to be successful in spiritual warfare, so much so that living an abundant Christian life largely depends on our ability to set aside time with God daily and communicate with Him. Both weapons of prayer and worship are mighty for redirecting our focus off of ourselves and onto the very nature of God—which is key to overcoming any type of spiritual battle.

Shifting atmospheres, which we will discuss in this chapter, is a technique that also provides this benefit. By using our gifts of discernment and finding out what God wants to release into our situations, we can partner with the Holy Spirit to release His presence into the spiritual realm and reject the enemy's voice.

Prayer and worship are so important, because when we connect with God and present to Him our needs, we position ourselves to rely on His goodness rather than our own abilities. Acknowledging God's sovereignty breaks the power of the enemy's lies and turns our attention to how big the Lord is in comparison to the threat at hand. In partnering with God and His perspective on our situation, our prayers and worship become a vibrant act of warfare.

THE WEAPON OF PRAYER

In Scripture, the Bible gives us countless verses on how to pray. One of my favorite verses on this subject comes from the apostle Paul in Philippians:

> *Do not be anxious about anything, but in everything by prayer and supplication with thanksgiving let your requests be made known to God. And the peace of God, which surpasses all understanding, will guard your hearts and your minds in Christ Jesus* (Philippians 4:6-7).

In this verse, Paul makes it clear we are to present our needs to God. Always. As our main source of communication with God, prayer establishes and maintains our partnership with Him and the spiritual realm. It acknowledges our need for His care in our lives and positions us for His blessing and protection. Prayer becomes a shield that aligns us under the protective wings of our heavenly Father. Although God already knows our needs and often answers our prayers before we even ask for them, the Bible reaffirms the importance of us daily communicating with Him (see Matt. 6:8; Phil. 4:6).

Another reason why we pray is because our enemies are not flesh and blood. The devil and his forces are spiritual, and often his attacks against us are based in the spiritual realm as well. The enemy can attack us in our flesh (through sickness) and even our soul (in the mind), but he can also hit us through attacks (fiery darts) in the spiritual realm that affect our bodies and thoughts.

We explored some of this in chapter 3 with body, soul, and spirit crossovers. Often when I pray for people, I find their physical and/or emotional issues have a spiritual component attached. For instance, if a person has been dabbling in the occult (through yoga, tarot cards, or crystals), it can open a spiritual door in their lives to the demonic realm. Negative spiritual ramifications develop as this door remains open. People in these situations may find themselves wondering why they have lost their peace, why they are experiencing nightmares, why their prayers are not being answered, or why they are being hit with unceasing physical or emotional attacks.

The enemy tries to trick us into thinking we are fighting the people next door or the political party that we happen to disagree with the most. The reality is we are facing spiritual powers and principalities that are at war against us. Prayer is one of the best ways we can activate God's truth into the unseen realm and cast down the enemy's attacks. The Bible says:

> *Finally, be strong in the Lord and in the strength of his might. Put on the whole armor of God, that you may be able to stand against the schemes of the devil. For we do not wrestle against flesh and blood, but against the rulers, against the authorities, against the cosmic powers over this present darkness, against the spiritual forces of evil in the heavenly places* (Ephesians 6:10-12).
>
> *For though we walk in the flesh, we are not waging war according to the flesh. For the weapons of our warfare are not of the flesh but have divine power to destroy strongholds. We destroy arguments and every lofty opinion raised against the knowledge of God, and take every thought captive to obey Christ* (2 Corinthians 10:3-5).

When we fight the people around us and fail to properly engage the spiritual realm, we render ourselves ineffective in tearing down the enemy's strongholds. This, obviously, is not the way we should do warfare.

This reminds me of a story my daughter-in-law, Colleen, told me several years ago. She had a dream in which she was inside an unfamiliar house with a small group of people. Somehow everyone knew there was a murderer inside lurking in the shadows. Everyone had their knives out ready to protect themselves, but because the house was pitch black, they couldn't see what was happening around them. Everyone ended up panicking and swinging their knives around trying to protect themselves. What they didn't realize was that they ended up accidentally stabbing each other in the process.

To me, this is exactly what happens when we battle unwisely. We intercede, judge, and blame people (or even God), and cut down others with our words when we should be rebuking the demonic spirits in the second heaven that are harassing us.

Prayer is a spiritual armor that protects us when we partner with God. When we cover ourselves and others in prayer, we are showing the enemy we are protected by Christ's blood. As we step into this promise, the devil is forced to abandon his desired attacks against us. Living our lives as Christians means we need to be constant in prayer and keep alert to what is really going on in the spiritual realm. If we hope to be successful in spiritual battle, we need to be adept at prayer.

PRAYING FOR OURSELVES

Prayer, like worship, is our direct line of communication with God. It is perhaps one of the most powerful weapons we have access to as believers. Because of this, the devil tries to discourage us from talking to the Father.

One of the most common ways the devil does this is by dissuading us from ever bringing up our needs before God. The enemy whispers lies like, "It's unhealthy to focus on our own needs and communicate them to God," "You should only pray for big issues," "God already remembers what you prayed for," or "You don't really need to pray again." Over and over, these lies get planted in our minds, and if we are not careful, they become unhealthy root systems of thought.

When we hear such thoughts from the enemy, we must learn to rebuke them immediately because they are in direct conflict with God's Scripture. All throughout God's Word, we are reminded that the Lord wants to hear from His children—and telling Him our needs is one of the great privileges that we have as His sons and daughters.

An example from Scripture that shows the importance of bringing our needs before the Father is the story of the wicked judge. In this story, a widow bothered a judge over and over to give her justice. Eventually, the judge gave into the woman's commands but it was not because he was a Christian. In fact, he did not even believe in God at all, but because he was so annoyed by the woman's pestering, he gave in to her demands (see Luke 18:1-8). How much greater of an influence do we have with our heavenly Father because He is righteous! That is the influence we carry in prayer.

We live in a tension where God already knows what we need, but because He longs to be in relationship with us, we are commanded to lay our hearts and desires before Him. When we pray, our answers get sent to us from the angelic realm so we can step into them here on earth. When the enemy says you shouldn't pray for yourself, remind him that, yes, it is legal to pray for your own needs. In fact, it is biblical. Consider this verse:

> *And this is the confidence that we have toward him, that if we ask anything according to his will he hears us. And if we know that he hears us in whatever we ask, we know that we have the requests that we have asked of him* (1 John 5:14-15).

PRAYING FOR OTHERS

Although it is important to pray for ourselves and our own needs, it is crucial we don't *just* pray for ourselves. If we only ever pray for ourselves and our own problems, then we are not using the weapon of prayer to its full potential. When we pray for others, we cover them with a blessing from God, shield them from the enemy, and uphold their weary arms. This is at the heart of intercessory prayer and is one of our primary callings as warriors for God.

In First Peter 5:8, we read, *"Be alert and of sober mind. Your enemy the devil prowls around like a roaring lion looking for someone to devour"* (NIV). Intercession is a type of prayer that declares, "I see your desire, enemy, to devour this person, but you are not going to be allowed to do so. I send you back in Jesus's name!"

Intercession is a gift from God that lifts up others in prayer. It places a shield of God's protection around them, releases Heaven's armies to do battle for them, and shields them from all manner of attack. Two excellent resources for this type of prayer are Beni Johnson's book, *The Happy Intercessor*, and Dutch Sheets's *Intercessory Prayer.*

PETITIONING PRAYER

A very specific type of intercessory prayer I use often is petitioning prayer. This is the type of prayer that postures me before God and says, "Help! I need You to fight this battle for me!"

It is important when doing petitioning prayers to not use silly repetition. God hears what we pray and knows what we need, so we can be confident in knowing He hears us when we cry out for His provision. Scripture says:

> *And when you pray, do not heap up empty phrases as the Gentiles do, for they think that they will be heard for their many words. Do not be like them, for your Father knows what you need before you ask him* (Matthew 6:7-8).

If we start our petitioning prayers from a place of fear, then we should stay with God and work to replace our fear with His peace. We can keep praying until we feel His peace that "surpasses all understanding" flow over us, and make sure His peace goes out with us and invades our situations (Phil. 4:7). It is important to note that our situations may not instantly change after praying, and sometimes they might even seem to get worse. But no matter how our circumstances look, they are being watched over by God's goodness and love for us.

No matter how scary our situations look or how unstable our lives may feel, God's peace can step in and shift our minds to His perspective. Once we train ourselves to be aligned with God's perspective, nothing will be able to shake us. We will realize that we are not under the enemy's hold but that we are seated with Christ in the heavenlies where satan is truly under our feet.

REMINDING PRAYER

Reminding God of His promises is a powerful way we can remind ourselves of the breakthroughs from Heaven that are coming. God never forgets what He has promised us, but we can sometimes find ourselves questioning what God has told us when life's problems get difficult.

If God has given us promises, and we feel they are still waiting to come true, we can get alone with Him and ask, "God, what promises are You wanting to show me today?" We can remind Him of the promises He has spoken over us and invite Him to step in and take His rightful place as our Savior who brings old dreams back to life.

Reminding prayer is a type of petitioning prayer that is first found in Second Samuel. It encourages us to align with God's perspective and asks the Lord to redeem the promises that have been waiting to take action in our lives. Let's read this passage:

> *And now, O Lord God, confirm forever the word that you have spoken concerning your servant and concerning his house, and do as you have spoken. And your name will be magnified forever, saying, "The Lord of Hosts is God over Israel," and the house of your servant David will be established before you* (2 Samuel 7:25-26).

Reminding God of who He is and His promises over us is not manipulative or self-indulgent. It is reminding ourselves and the spiritual realm that God is still King— even when our circumstances don't reflect that truth.

Praying like this might seem difficult. It might even seem sacrilegious, but it is still petitioning prayer. It is us asking God to come through, but doing so in such a way that reminds Him (and our spirits) about all the promises He has already fulfilled in our lives. In a way, it is a testimony-fueled type of prayer, pushing out God's goodness into the atmospheres and inviting future breakthrough.

The reminding prayer is also a wonderful way to gird ourselves in the truths of God's testimonies. Reminding ourselves and God of all the promises He has fulfilled, we prepare ourselves to see all the coming breakthroughs God is willing to make happen.

I learned this concept early with our Pastor Bill Johnson of Bethel Church. Bill loves to teach on the value of this type of prayer. Bill has told us many times that he brings a binder full of God's promises with him wherever he goes. Whenever he gets discouraged, he simply looks through the words God has given him and speaks them into fruition. It is a way for Bill to spiritually fortify himself against the enemy's attacks. For the past thirty years, it has helped him immensely to navigate through painful seasons in life.[1]

As you grow in your understanding of prayer, realize that reminding prayers are extremely powerful. Remembering what God has said over you reminds you of His promises and encourages you where you are going in Christ. As an act of warfare, these types of prayers declare into the spiritual realm what God has already done and reminds your spirit of the breakthroughs that are soon to come.

DECLARATION PRAYERS

Another type of prayer I like to use often are declarative prayers. These are prayers that are not asking God for our needs to be met, but are instead declaring them into the atmosphere as though they are already being met. Declarative prayers are us speaking out what God has already said and partnering with them as an act of faith.

Declaration prayers are essentially us saying, "God, I know You said Jehovah Rapha is the healer, so I am handing You this sickness and declaring that You, God, are my healer. Thank You for healing me in Jesus's name."

We begin declarative prayers by declaring truths that are found in God's Word. We apply them to our circumstances and then speak them into existence. When we feel hemmed in on every side, declaration prayers are a great way to reassure ourselves we are not alone.

When you use declarative prayers, you declare prophetically into the spiritual realm what you already know. You activate God's promises in your life and bring them into fruition. You can even add a little twist on this and make it a commanding prayer. This type of prayer can be seen in Mark:

> *Truly, I say to you, whoever says to this moun-*
> *tain, "Be taken up and thrown into the sea,"*
> *and does not doubt in his heart, but believes that*
> *what he says will come to pass, it will be done for*
> *him. Therefore I tell you, whatever you ask in*
> *prayer, believe that you have received it, and it*
> *will be yours* (Mark 11:23-24).

Pastor Danny Silk once told me that while he was ministering to a church, he put a mustard seed on his finger, held it out in front of the crowd, and said, "Hey, I've got a mustard seed and I'm not afraid to use it!" Faith and fearless devotion is the power of declarative and commanding prayers. I use these types of prayers a lot in the deliverance ministry. When I pray for someone, I say, "No, enemy, you have to bow. I see you, discouragement (whatever they are fighting), and I command you to be silent in Jesus's name."

Declaration and commanding prayers are great ways to take authority over the spiritual realm and tell the enemy, "No way!" If you find yourself in scary situations, use these prayers, and watch as God shifts your circumstances for good.

INQUIRY PRAYER

Another type of prayer I use often is inquiry prayer. Inquiry prayer differs from prayers of petition in that we are not telling God our needs but rather listening to Him speak to us. Inquiry prayer is not us asking God to meet our needs, but rather us coming before Him and asking what He thinks of our situation. It is the type of prayer I see as intimate, quiet, and revelatory. Here is what the Scriptures say regarding inquiry prayer:

> *This is how one should regard us, as servants*
> *of Christ and stewards of the mysteries of God*
> (1 Corinthians 4:1).

"Stewards of the mysteries of God"—ask yourself what this phrase means and ponder what being a steward of the mysteries of God looks like. Is there even such a thing called a mystery of God? If so, how do we steward it, and how do we find it out?

Inquiry prayer is unique in that it requires us to come boldly before the throne, and yet carefully handle this privilege with honor. In real life, nobody ever comes to a king, a president, or some other nation's ruler without some understanding of protocol, title, or grace. Inquiry prayer works in this same way. God is our King and our Father, but He is also the Creator of the universe. Although we are allowed through Christ to boldly approach the throne, we need to enter God's presence with the reverence He deserves.

There is a time for bold declarative prayers, but there is also a time for quiet prayers that rest in God's presence. The Old Testament has many verses where kings, prophets, and priests inquired of the Lord about how to engage the enemy (see 1 Sam. 22:10; 2 Sam. 2:1). King Josiah asked his priests to inquire of the Lord for wisdom concerning the proper way to follow God's laws (see 2 Chron. 34:19-28). King David asked God throughout his life about how to do battle against his enemies. I believe inquiry prayer is one of the reasons why Solomon was so wise. He understood how to come before the Lord and ask for His wisdom. He saw prayer as an opportunity not to just connect with God, but to also see His mysteries revealed.

Great battle strategies will be revealed as we lean more into this type of prayer. As stewards of God's mysteries, we will begin to see faster and more powerful breakthrough in our lives. As we grow in our understanding of warfare, we must learn to master this type of prayer.

THE WEAPON OF WORSHIP: FRONTLINE WARFARE

Another weapon of warfare God gives us is worship, and it truly is a powerful act. Throughout Scripture, God's people used worship as a weapon, and in order to war wisely, we need to understand the powerful, spiritual ramifications of worshipping God. I believe the more we worship, the weaker the devil becomes.

The Bible says we *"enter his gates with thanksgiving and his courts with praise"* (Ps. 100:4 NIV). As the Creator of Heaven and Earth, God is the most powerful being to ever exist. Worship is the simple act of us acknowledging His sovereignty and positioning ourselves in submission to Him. God does not require us to worship Him because He is envious, insecure, or demanding. We worship Him because He is due the glory. Consider this passage from Scripture that expresses God's holiness:

> *Around the throne were twenty-four thrones, and seated on the thrones were twenty-four elders, clothed in white garments, with golden crowns on their heads. From the throne came flashes of lightning, and rumblings and peals of thunder, and before the throne were burning seven torches of fire, which are the seven spirits of God, and before the throne there was as it were a sea of glass, like crystal. And around the throne, on each side of the throne, are four living creatures....and day and night they never cease to*

say, "Holy, holy, holy, is the Lord God Almighty, who was and is and is to come!" And whenever the living creatures give glory and honor and thanks to him who is seated on the throne, who lives forever and ever, the twenty-four elders fall down before him who is seated on the throne and worship him who lives forever and ever. They cast their crowns before the throne, saying, "Worthy are you, our Lord and God, to receive glory and honor and power, for you created all things, and by your will they existed and were created" (Revelation 4:4-6, 8-11).

Worship is our response to acknowledging God's glory. Simply comprehending His goodness elicits this response in us, and when we focus on God and how wonderful He is, the attacks from the enemy take a lesser role in our focus. When we are engaged in spiritual warfare, we must keep our eyes focused on the Lord—for He is truly the supreme being. As we stare into His eyes, all other troubles fade.

WORSHIPPING IN BATTLE

One of my favorite stories from Scripture that shows the importance of worship is during the reign of Jehoshaphat. When the enemies of Judah, the Moabites and Meunites amassed against God's people, King Jehoshaphat went to God and asked Him for a winning strategy. Scripture says:

After this the Moabites and Ammonites, and with them some of the Meunites, came against

Jehoshaphat for battle. Some men came and told Jehoshaphat, "A great multitude is coming against you from Edom, from beyond the sea; and, behold, they are in Hazazon-tamar" (that is, Engedi). *Then Jehoshaphat was afraid and set his face to seek the Lord, and proclaimed a fast throughout all Judah* (2 Chronicles 20:1-3).

Jehoshaphat brought his fears to God and asked Him what He wanted to do about his situation. Instead of giving into fear, Jehoshaphat turned to God and submitted to Him in prayer. Bringing his concerns before God, Jehoshaphat heard God's winning strategy. This teaches us that refocusing on God will always change our perspective on the battle.

Interestingly, the Lord's winning strategy wasn't to add more troops or to invest in better technology. Instead, God commanded Jehoshaphat and his generals to go out and face the enemy because the Lord would do battle for them. Consider this verse below:

And the Spirit of the Lord came upon Jahaziel the son of Zechariah, son of Benaiah, son of Jeiel, son of Mattaniah, a Levite of the sons of Asaph, in the midst of the assembly. And he said, "Listen, all Judah and inhabitants of Jerusalem and King Jehoshaphat: Thus says the Lord to you, 'Do not be afraid and do not be dismayed at this great horde, for the battle is not yours but God's. Tomorrow go down against them. Behold, they

*will come up by the ascent of Ziz. You will find
them at the end of the valley, east of the wilderness of Jeruel '"* (2 Chronicles 20:14-16).

Notice that the Lord did not instantly bring about the
Moabites' destruction. He simply gave Judah a command,
and the armies of Jehoshaphat had to be obedient and follow
through. Where this story gets interesting is that instead of
sending the cavalry or infantrymen up front, Jehoshaphat
sent his worshippers. In what can be considered one of the
most absurd winning war strategies in history, Jehoshaphat
put his musicians and singers in the front lines, and amazingly, this single act turned the tide of battle. Consider
this passage:

*And when he had taken counsel with the people,
he appointed those who were to sing to the Lord
and praise him in holy attire, as they went before
the army, and say, "Give thanks to the Lord, for
his steadfast love endures forever." And when
they began to sing and praise, the Lord set an
ambush against the men of Ammon, Moab, and
Mount Seir, who had come against Judah, so that
they were routed. For the men of Ammon and
Moab rose against the inhabitants of Mount Seir,
devoting them to destruction, and when they had
made an end of the inhabitants of Seir, they all
helped to destroy one another. When Judah came
to the watchtower of the wilderness, they looked
toward the horde, and behold, there were dead*

*bodies lying on the ground; none had escaped.
When Jehoshaphat and his people came to take
their spoil, they found among them, in great
numbers, goods, clothing, and precious things,
which they took for themselves until they could
carry no more. They were three days in taking the
spoil, it was so much* (2 Chronicles 20:21-25).

As I read this passage, it encourages me that my problems are not bigger than God. It reassures me that as I turn to Him and acknowledge His goodness, faithfulness and might, the enemy is put in his place. I might feel overwhelmed and defeated in the moment, but as I worship, my focus will shift off of the strength of the enemy and onto God.

Here are some other examples from Scripture that show worship being used as a weapon of warfare:

*And at the seventh time, when the priests had
blown the trumpets, Joshua said to the people,
"Shout, for the Lord has given you the city. And
the city and all that is within it shall be devoted
to the Lord for destruction. Only Rahab the pros-
titute and all who are with her in her house
shall live, because she hid the messengers whom
we sent."…So the people shouted, and the trumpets were blown. As soon as the people heard the
sound of the trumpet, the people shouted a great
shout, and the wall fell down flat, so that the
people went up into the city, every man straight*

before him, and they captured the city. Then they devoted all in the city to destruction, both men and women, young and old, oxen, sheep, and donkeys, with the edge of the sword (Joshua 6:16-17, 20-21).

But when her owners saw that their hope of gain was gone, they seized Paul and Silas and dragged them into the marketplace before the rulers. And when they had brought them to the magistrates, they said, "These men are Jews, and they are disturbing our city. They advocate customs that are not lawful for us as Romans to accept or practice." The crowd joined in attacking them, and the magistrates tore the garments off them and gave orders to beat them with rods. And when they had inflicted many blows upon them, they threw them into prison, ordering the jailer to keep them safely. Having received this order, he put them into the inner prison and fastened their feet in the stocks. About midnight Paul and Silas were praying and singing hymns to God, and the prisoners were listening to them, and suddenly there was a great earthquake, so that the foundations of the prison were shaken. And immediately all the doors were opened, and everyone's bonds were unfastened (Acts 16:19-26).

As you grow in your understanding of spiritual warfare, I want to encourage you to cultivate the habit of daily worshipping the Lord. As an act of warfare, praise ushers in the presence of God. It confuses the enemy and prepares your heart for God's rescue. Partnering with worship, you position yourself for God's goodness and watch as His Spirit takes preeminence. Consider this verse from Scripture:

> *Then he* [the angel] *said to me, "This is the word of the Lord to Zerubbabel: Not by might, nor by power, but by my Spirit, says the Lord of Hosts"* (Zechariah 4:6).

As we move forward into this next season, I want to encourage you. Your victories will not come as you work out of your own strength, but as you partner with God and release His Spirit through prayer and worship. The true battle belongs to the Lord.

THE WEAPON OF SHIFTING ATMOSPHERES

If you want a more in-depth look at this weapon of warfare, check out my second book, *Shifting Atmospheres*. It is a thorough guide that explores this weapon at a practical, easy-to-understand level. For those who are new to the concept, shifting atmospheres is simply an easy way for you to partner with Jesus and use your gift of discernment to discover what is going on in the spiritual realm around you. It lays out a helpful strategy so you can partner with God and remove any negative atmospheres you are discerning. Once you identify their holds and reject their influence, you can partner with God to release His broadcasts in their place. It is an insightful biblical tool I use often and is one I hope you find useful as well.

When I teach about shifting atmospheres around the globe, I tell people the best way to learn this strategy is to think about how radio stations work in your car. Each station has its own list of songs. Some stations play tunes that are loud and are filled with lyrics about violence and/or sexual exploitation. Other stations play mellow and relaxing love songs. When we tune into a station we don't like, we simply change the channel. This is similar to what happens when we "pick up" enemy broadcasts and learn to switch the channel and see what God wants us to release into the atmosphere instead.

As Christians, we should be walking transmitters of the Holy Spirit. We should only be emitting the sounds and atmospheres that resonate with Heaven. When we tune ourselves to Heaven's broadcasts, it becomes easy to discern what the enemy is doing. Messages from the enemy sound harsh and loud to our ears (Paul likens the enemy's voice to a noisy gong in First Corinthians 13:1).

Whenever I travel and speak in other regions, I try to discern what is being broadcast into the spiritual atmosphere. If I discern fear, hate, or suicide, I partner with the church's leaders to renounce the spirits and release God's presence in their place. Understanding what the enemy is broadcasting gives me a glimpse into the enemy's camp and allows me to cancel his assignments and begin releasing God's voice over the region instead.

When you walk into your church, home, workplace, or a public store, get in the habit of asking yourself what is going on in the spiritual realm. Before you step inside, take an inventory of how you feel. Are you happy or sad, afraid or excited? Check out how you feel when entering a room. See what has changed. Pay attention to the spiritual broadcasts you are picking up. As you practice, you will increase your discernment and begin to take authority over your own mind by simply "changing the channel."

CONCLUSION

Using God's spiritual weapons is important when facing off against spiritual enemies. Connecting to God's nature through prayer, worship, and tools like shifting atmospheres can help you activate your spirit and do warfare correctly.

In the next three chapters, we will look at some other powerful weapons—such as connecting with God's nature through His names listed in Scripture and applying these names so we can see His goodness invade our situations.

SUMMARY

POINT TO PONDER

There are many types of prayers to wield as weapons of warfare. Be familiar with each one and ask the Holy Spirit when to step out into each one of them. Worship and shifting atmospheres are also mighty weapons you can wield.

VERSE TO REMEMBER

Rejoice always, pray without ceasing, give thanks in all circumstances; for this is the will of God in Christ Jesus for you.
—1 Thessalonians 5:16-18

QUESTIONS TO CONSIDER

1. Is there a type of prayer listed in this chapter that you are not familiar with?

2. What is your favorite type of prayer?

3. Is there another type of prayer you use that is not listed in this book?

4. What worship songs are resonating with you in this season?

5. Do you have a proper understanding of how to discern what is going on around you in the spirit realm?

6. Have you learned to effectively shift the atmospheres in your life?

PRAYER

Thank You, Jesus, for showing me so many different ways to pray. Teach me how to connect with You more so that I can mightily wield the weapons of prayer and worship. I invite your Spirit to invade my life. Teach me secrets and the mysteries of God. I can't wait to hear the treasures You will share with me.

ACTIVATION

Ask the Lord to show you which types of prayer you should be practicing more. Ask the Holy Spirit to prompt you throughout your week to pray however He reveals. Take time in your daily routine to stop and worship God and record how situations in your life begin to change. Practice discerning what is going on around you in the spiritual realm and ask God what He wants you to release into the atmosphere.

NOTE

1. "Stewarding the Prophetic," Bethel TV video, posted August 2010, https://www.bethel.tv/watch/729.

CHAPTER 7

HIS NAME, HIS NATURE (PART 1)

The name of the Lord is a fortified tower;
the righteous run to it and are safe.
—PROVERBS 18:10 NIV

Pastor Graham Cooke has a wonderful question to ask God: "Lord, what is it You want to be for me now that this is happening that You couldn't be at any other time.... What is it You want to be for me? Who do You want to be for me in this?"[1] Reminding ourselves of God's nature is not a distant, biblical concept, but a powerful weapon we can use in battle to bring encouragement to our daily lives. When we face financial difficulties, for example, we can turn to Jehovah Jireh, the Lord Who Provides. When we struggle with fear or anxiety, we can call upon Jehovah Sabaoth, the Lord of Hosts.

Since God is the same yesterday, today, and tomorrow, we can stand in the truth of who He is in Scripture and declare His blessings over us. Many of the names of God are found in the Old Testament, but that does not mean they are not relevant today. Connecting with God's nature not only allows us to pull on His goodness, it also takes our eyes off the enemy and puts them back on the Lord where they belong.

So much about us winning in spiritual warfare is dependent on us putting our eyes back on God. When we focus on the enemy, we become weak and vulnerable. When we focus on the Lord, our spirits soar.

Because God has so many unique attributes, we will be discussing them over the course of the next three chapters. But for the sake of time, only a handful of God's names will be discussed. Once you finish this book, I suggest you do your own private study on the names of God.

Be sure to ask God as you read through these chapters which names He wants you to connect with for your current situation. Maybe you are experiencing chaos in your life and you need to hear from Jehovah Shalom, the God of Peace. Or maybe you are feeling invisible and need to hear from Jehovah Roi, the God Who Sees.

Also, realize that each of these names are not solely focused on Father God. Jesus and the Holy Spirit are included too. Jesus came as a direct representation of the Father, so each of these names from the Old Testament reveals His nature as well. The best part about learning all this is that as you pursue Father God and tap into His nature, your relationship with Jesus and Holy Spirit will improve as well. Consider this verse:

> *"If you had known me, you would have known my Father also. From now on you do know him and have seen him." Philip said to him, "Lord, show us the Father, and it is enough for us." Jesus said to him, "Have I been with you so long, and you still do not know me, Philip? Whoever has seen me has seen the Father. How can you say, 'Show us the Father'? Do you not believe that I am in the Father and the Father is in Me? The words that I say to you I do not speak on my own authority, but the Father who dwells in me does his works. Believe me that I am in the Father and the Father is in me, or else believe on account of the works themselves"* (John 14:7-11).

JEHOVAH TSIDKENU

For He made Him who knew no sin to be sin for us, that we might become the righteousness of God in Him (2 Corinthians 5:21 NKJV).

One of names of God I value most is Jehovah Tsidkenu, the Lord Our Righteousness. This is the name of God that reminds me I am covered by His grace and mercy because my sins are forgiven through the blood of Christ. Partnering with my identity in Christ, I can stand boldly before God's throne and know in Him I am loved and protected.

The name Jehovah Tsidkenu is first used in Jeremiah. Here is the passage below:

> *"The days are coming," declares the Lord, "when I will raise up for David a righteous Branch, a King who will reign wisely and do what is just and right in the land. In his days Judah will be saved and Israel will live in safety. This is the name by which he will be called: The Lord Our Righteous Savior"* (Jeremiah 23:5-6 NIV).

The word *righteous* in this passage translates as: "just, righteous (in conduct and character)" and "righteous (as justified and vindicated by God)."[2] Jesus, David's "righteous Branch," is prophesied to act in accordance with God's divine and moral law. As a person who has lived without sin and represents grace and purity, Jesus serves as our perfect sacrifice. His sacrifice and willingness to become sin so we can become free liberates us so we no longer have to live beneath the enemy's power. Through His death and resurrection, Jesus purchased for us an immeasurable gift of righteousness—one that we can still lean on to this day.

Today, when we confess our sins and call upon the name of the Lord, His righteousness covers us and sets us in right moral standing with the Father. Voices bringing guilt and shame have no power as we become hidden in the redemption of Christ, the Lord our Righteousness (see Heb. 4:16).

When the enemy screams and says, "You don't deserve to be rescued," remind him of who Jehovah Tsidkenu is— your righteousness—and walk in that identity.

WALKING IN RIGHTEOUSNESS

What would it look like if we actually believed we were covered in the Lord's righteousness? How would we behave? How would we act differently? What would happen if we believed we were under Jesus's protection from guilt and shame? I'm willing to think our lives would look much different. Here are some hints from Scripture that show us how our lives could be:

> *We know that our old self was crucified with him [Jesus] in order that the body of sin might be brought to nothing, so that we would no longer be enslaved to sin. For one who has died has been set free from sin* (Romans 6:6-7).

> *There is therefore now no condemnation for those who are in Christ Jesus. For the law of the Spirit of life has set you free in Christ Jesus from the law of sin and death* (Romans 8:1-2).

> *For those whom he foreknew he also predestined to be conformed to the image of his Son, in order that he might be the firstborn among many*

brothers. And those whom he predestined he also called, and those whom he called he also justified, and those whom he justified he also glorified (Romans 8:29-30).

In these verses, the Bible explains we are free from condemnation. All our past sins have been erased. We have become new creations in Christ raised up to be seated with Him in the heavenlies.

When the enemy says, "God may have been your righteousness yesterday, but you messed up so bad today that you're no longer in His grace," confess your sins to God and allow Jesus's righteousness to pour over your situation. Realize the enemy has no power over you unless you allow it. Bathe yourself in God's mercy and reject the enemy's voice—because you have been covered by Jesus's righteousness!

Because we are new creations in Christ, the lies that previously told us we were enslaved to sin have no power. They are simply tricks trying to pull us back into our old lives. We need to remind ourselves daily that after Jesus came into our hearts, our old lives of sin were crucified and buried. Consider this verse:

If we confess our sins, He is faithful and righteous to forgive us our sins and to cleanse us from all unrighteousness (1 John 1:9 NASB).

We know that Christ, being raised from the dead, will never die again; death no longer has dominion over him. For the death he died he died to

sin, once for all, but the life he lives he lives to
God. So you also must consider yourselves dead
to sin and alive to God in Christ Jesus (Romans
6:9-11).

Take some time right now and thank the Lord for being
your righteousness. Ask Him to break you free from the
mocking accusations of the enemy: any condemnation,
guilt, shame, performance, and/or works. Renounce any
partnerships with fear, rejection, or failure. Renounce any
lies you are believing about yourself and hand them to Jesus
once and for all. Release your past into the hands of Jehovah Tsidkenu and ask for His righteousness. After you have
prayed through all this, stand in your new identity of righteousness as you receive God's love.

Here are some more verses that can help you when you
are hearing the enemy's voice:

I am the Lord; I have called you in righteous-
ness; I will take you by the hand and keep you; I
will give you as a covenant for the people, a light
for the nations, to open the eyes that are blind,
to bring out the prisoners from the dungeon,
from the prison those who sit in darkness (Isaiah
42:6-7).

My dear children, I am writing this to you so
that you will not sin. But if anyone does sin, we
have an advocate who pleads our case before the
Father. He is Jesus Christ, the one who is truly
righteous. He himself is the sacrifice that atones

for our sins—and not only our sins but the sins of all the world (1 John 2:1-2 NLT).

The enemy so badly does not want you to comprehend the depth of Jesus's righteousness over you. If the enemy can get you to question God's forgiveness of your past, then you will shy away from your true identity as a victorious overcomer.

When you understand the fullness of what Christ did for you, then you will be at peace knowing that through Jesus you are accepted. Because of Christ's blood, you have been made perfect and renewed. The enemy has no power over you unless you allow it. Scripture says:

> *For by grace you have been saved through faith. And this is not your own doing; it is the gift of God, not as a result of works, so that no one may boast* (Ephesians 2:8-9).

> *So then, since we have a great High Priest who has entered heaven, Jesus the Son of God, let us hold firmly to what we believe. This High Priest of ours understands our weaknesses, for he faced all of the same testings we do, yet he did not sin. So let us come boldly to the throne of our gracious God. There we will receive his mercy, and we will find grace to help us when we need it most* (Hebrews 4:14-16 NLT).

What would happen if you actually believed Jesus is your righteousness? How would your life be different?

Guilt and shame would bow. Fear and isolation would have no power. Every hindrance to your connection with God would be destroyed. Remember, because of what Jesus did, the enemy has no power over you.

When you are feeling discouraged and overwhelmed by your past sin, remember that Jesus is your advocate before the Father—and rest in the fact that *He* is your righteousness.

JEHOVAH RAPHA

Jesus was going through all the cities and villages, teaching in their synagogues and proclaiming the gospel of the kingdom, and healing every kind of disease and every kind of sickness (Matthew 9:35 NASB).

Another name of God I like to connect with often is Jehovah Rapha, the healer. This is the name of God I call upon when I am experiencing pain, heartbreak, or physical infirmity. When I am struggling with physical issues, I ask Jehovah Rapha, the God Who Heals, for His healing touch to come in and redeem my situation. Here is this name first used in Scripture:

If you will diligently listen to the voice of the Lord your God, and do that which is right in his eyes, and give ear to his commandments and keep all his statutes, I will put none of the diseases on you that I put on the Egyptians, for I am the Lord, your healer (Exodus 15:26).

"For I am the Lord, your healer." Not many verses encourage me more than this. If we look through Scripture, we will see the Bible is full of verses that show God's desire to heal. In fact, I would go so far as to say it is within His nature to do so. If we look at Jesus's life and His time in ministry, Jesus didn't heal some or even most of those people who came to Him. Jesus healed them all.

Jesus, the physical representation of God, went through His life destroying the works of the enemy and reminding people that their heavenly Father was a God of love who deeply cared about them. Just look at these verses below and see how Jehovah Rapha's healing touch fills our body, soul, and spirit. Through the Holy Spirit, Jesus was able to remove sickness, disease, dread, and torment. Opening the door to Jesus and Jehovah Rapha's touch is another benefit of being a child of God. Because of Jesus's sacrifice, we have access to this divine gift. Whenever we are struggling with pain and other physical issues, we can turn to Jehovah Rapha, the God Who Heals, and ask for His healing touch to step in and change our projected outcome. Consider these verses:

> *And a leper came to Him and bowed down before Him, and said, "Lord, if You are willing, You can make me clean." Jesus stretched out His hand and touched him, saying, "I am willing; be cleansed." And immediately his leprosy was cleansed* (Matthew 8:2-3 NASB).

Worship the Lord your God, and his blessing will be on your food and water. I will take away sickness from among you (Exodus 23:25 NIV).

For the Lord protects the bones of the righteous; not one of them is broken! (Psalm 34:20 NLT)

He sent out his word and healed them, and delivered them from their destruction (Psalm 107:20).

"I have seen what they do, but I will heal them anyway! I will lead them. I will comfort those who mourn, bringing words of praise to their lips. May they have abundant peace, both near and far," says the Lord, who heals them (Isaiah 57:18-19 NLT).

Heal me, O Lord, and I shall be healed; save me, and I shall be saved, for You are my praise (Jeremiah 17:14 NKJV).

He [Jesus] *said to her, "Daughter, your faith has healed you. Go in peace and be freed from your suffering"* (Mark 5:34 NIV).

And he laid his hands on her, and immediately she was made straight, and she glorified God (Luke 13:13).

And now, Lord, look upon their threats and grant to your servants to continue to speak your word with all boldness, while you stretch out your hand to heal, and signs and wonders are performed through the name of your holy servant Jesus (Acts 4:29-30).

And Peter said to him, "Aeneas, Jesus Christ heals you; rise and make your bed." And immediately he rose (Acts 9:34).

I remember the first time I was called up to the front to pray for people who were sick. I was terrified because I was convinced I wouldn't have the right words or proper technique to get them healed. As I stood at the front of the church, I silently prayed God would send me someone with a headache or slight cough. But of course, the first person who approached me had terminal cancer. I screamed inside and pleaded with God to bring someone more anointed than me to pray for him.

Sadly, the person left without any sign of improvement, but I did learn a valuable lesson. If I was going to survive in this ministry, I'd need to realize a person's healing was not dependent upon my ability to pray correctly. I am simply called to be a faithful servant. My obedience and willingness to follow God is my responsibility. Jehovah Rapha, the God Who Heals, handles the rest.

GOD'S DESIRE TO HEAL

Today, whenever I pray for the sick, I remind myself Jehovah Rapha, the healer, is present to heal. I tell everyone Jesus desires to see them healed and that it is His very nature to do so. I have witnessed so many healings in my life as I have called upon the healer, Jesus, that I have no doubt it is His will for all of us to walk free spiritually, physically, and emotionally. Since healer is one of God's names, it does not surprise me that He heals often and that He loves to do so. I see physical healing and redemption as simply a reality of His nature.

A few years ago, a woman came up to me in the middle of a conference. I was sitting in the back monitoring the product and honestly was pretty tired from a long day of teaching. When the woman asked me if I remembered her, I said, "I'm sorry. I really don't. I have no recollection of you."

Undeterred, the woman said, "That's OK. I really didn't expect you to remember. The last time you saw me was about five years ago. I was battling stage four cancer. You were sitting in the back of the Sozo seminar working on emails while Teresa was finishing her teaching. I wasn't going to bother you at first, but then I thought, 'Why not? This is my only chance to have her pray for me.' I interrupted you and asked you to pray for me. You stood up, smiled, laid your hand on my shoulder, and said, 'Be healed.' At that moment, I felt the power of God shoot through my entire body, and I knew in that instant I was healed! So I want to thank you for letting me interrupt you and tell you that since then, not only have I not had any cancer, but I have also not had any allergies or colds."

In this inspiring testimony, God stepped in and healed the woman instantly. All I did was say a quick prayer and put my hand on her shoulder. Testimonies like these remind me that miracles still happen today and that often, it has nothing to do with the person praying other than their willingness to be obedient to God.

Many times, however, I find healing manifests over a longer period of time. As we hold onto the truth of God's nature, healing occurs, though it might take days, weeks, or even years. Holding onto God's truth may look like us confronting old mindsets that have held us back. For instance, we may believe being sick is just a part of human life. Until we remove this lie, our subconscious brains actually partner with the sickness, and our attitude of acceptance may block our ability to grab ahold of God's truth that He wants us to be healed.

Sometimes our physical issues seem insurmountable. They represent a physical or spiritual barrier we are facing, and we unknowingly give in to the lie that they will always be there no matter what. In these times, I tell people to connect to Father God and get His perspective on the situation. As they do, I have them command their diseases to come and stand before Jehovah Rapha, the God Who Heals. Usually this gives people the proper perspective over the issues they are facing. They realize their sicknesses are so small in comparison to God, and it immediately ignites in them a hope that positions them for healing.

Now, again, this is not me saying our minds or will can heal us. If that were the case, getting healed would simply be mind over matter. But I would like to suggest our negative attitudes can block God's ability to intervene. We saw it in Scripture when Jesus tried to minister in His hometown. The people's doubt blocked Him from doing any major miracles there (see Matt. 13:58).

This shows us that the power of our thoughts can have an effect on our lives. If you are in a season when you are struggling physically, partner with God and ask Him to reveal if there are any negative mindsets holding your sicknesses in place, then allow the Holy Spirit to step in and root them out.

After preaching a message about this, I walked the congregation through prayers renouncing mindsets they had previously held onto about God not wanting or not being able to heal them. The next day, we received an email from a young woman who stated, "I prayed those prayers last night, and when I woke up this morning, all my scars from self-harm were gone."

Although I do not know the specific lies this young woman had been believing, her healing manifested after she walked through breaking them off of her life. Sometimes all we need to do is get the proper perspective on our situations. Removing the lies we are believing about our situations and inviting Jesus to come and heal us may be all we need to give us hope that we too can experience breakthrough.

This is a reality I experienced when working with a man who was struggling with mental illness. Years ago, while I was on a plane flying back home to Redding, California, I struck up a conversation with the gentleman sitting next to me, and it quickly turned into a time of ministry.

This man appeared to be around sixty years old and seemed to be walking under a dark cloud of depression. Being polite, I asked him how he was doing and why he was on this flight.

The man said, "I am not doing very well. I've been on anti-depressant medication for over twenty years, and it has helped me stay sane. But when my new doctor realized how long I have been taking the medication, he told me he needs to get me off of them because it isn't good for me physically. I know I can't stay sane without these pills because prior to finding the right medication, I had battled horrendous depression. So I have come to say goodbye to my daughter and check in with the psych ward so they can help break my dependency on these drugs."

As we talked, I asked the man if I could pray for him and help him break free from the spirit of depression.

"Sure," the man said. "Why not? Let's try it."

"Alright," I said. "Picture yourself standing next to Father God."

The man sat there for a few moments in silence, eyes closed.

"Are you standing next to Him?"

"Yes," he said.

"Now, command the spirit of depression to come stand next to Father God. What do you see?"

"Wow," He said. "Depression is a lot bigger than God."

Voila! In this simple exchange, we had found the lie that was holding him in bondage. We spent the next twenty minutes of the flight breaking this mindset and revealing God's truth. By the time we had landed, the man saw the spirit of depression as nothing more than a harmless puddle on the floor.

It has been years since this encounter, and I have not heard back from this man to check up on his progress, but as he left the plane, he laughed and said, "When I go to my psych evaluation tomorrow, I probably shouldn't tell the doctor I was talking to God on the plane."

He left our meeting joyful and encouraged and full of hope that God was going to come through.

CONCLUSION

Both Jehovah Tsidkenu and Jehovah Rapha are powerful names of God we can use in spiritual battle. If you are feeling discouraged by your past, turn to Jehovah Tsidkenu, the God of Righteousness, and remind yourself that you are covered by Christ's blood. If you are struggling with physical issues, turn to Jehovah Rapha, the God Who Heals, and allow His healing touch to pour over your body, soul, and spirit. As you rest in these two characteristics of God, hope will begin to fill your spirit and release new life.

Summary

Point to Ponder

Jesus Christ bought your life out of satan's hand by His blood. If you have accepted Jesus as your Savior, you are redeemed. This redemption removes the stench of prior sin in your life and allows you bold access to the Father and Holy Spirit. But it doesn't stop there. Jesus wants to partner with you daily to dispel the enemy's darkness. He wants you to bring His truth, wisdom, and revelation into every season you encounter.

Verse to Remember

*Departing, they began going through
the villages, preaching the gospel
and healing everywhere.*
—Luke 9:6 NASB

Questions to Consider

1. Do you still struggle with shame even after confessing your sin?

2. Are you constantly trying to prove that you deserve God's love?

3. Do you believe God still heals today?

4. Are you struggling with a physical illness?

PRAYER

Thank You, Jesus, for purchasing me with Your precious blood. I declare that I am bought and paid for. The enemy has no hold over me. I stand in Your victory today.

ACTIVATION

Ask Jesus to take you to the Father and ask Father God what He thinks of you. Ask Him to remove sin from your life and reclothe you in the righteousness of Christ. If you are struggling to overcome sickness or physical issues, command these problems to stand next to Father God. See how small and insignificant they appear to His size.

NOTES

1. Graham Cooke, "Your Life Isn't Tough for God," YouTube, September 9, 2019, https://www.youtube.com/watch?v=D5EGXVI1Cuo.

2. Blue Letter Bible, s.v. "righteous," accessed February 4, 2020, https://www.blueletterbible.org/lang/lexicon/lexicon.cfm?Strongs=H6662&t=KJV.

CHAPTER 8

His Name, His Nature (Part II)

Ordering the people to sit down on the
grass, He took the five loaves and the two
fish, and looking up toward heaven, He
blessed the food, and breaking the loaves
He gave them to the disciples, and the
disciples gave them to the crowds.
—Matthew 14:19 NASB

Another of my favorite names of God to connect with is Jehovah Jireh, the Lord Will Provide. This is the name of God I call on when my physical needs (food, shelter, or finances) are not being met, and when my personal finances, emotional needs, and spiritual desires are lacking in break-through. In these times, I turn to Jehovah Jireh and ask Him to come through and provide for my situation.

Partnering with this name is key to winning battles in spiritual warfare, because when I partner with God's aspect of provision, it takes my focus off of whatever is wrong with my situation, and puts it back on what is right with God— my provider.

THE LORD WILL PROVIDE

The Bible makes it clear that our heavenly Father is the one who is responsible for providing our needs. Even though we can contribute to our own success through hard work, every blessing we receive is ultimately because of God's goodness. Consider this famous passage from Scripture:

> *Look at the birds. They don't plant or harvest or store food in barns, for your heavenly Father feeds them. And aren't you far more valuable to him than they are? Can all your worries add a single moment to your life? And why worry about your clothing? Look at the lilies of the field and how they grow. They don't work or make their clothing, yet Solomon in all his glory was not dressed as beautifully as they are. And if God cares so wonderfully for wildflowers that are here today and thrown into the fire tomorrow, he will certainly care for you. Why do you*

have so little faith? So don't worry about these things, saying, "What will we eat? What will we drink? What will we wear?" These things dominate the thoughts of unbelievers, but your heavenly Father already knows all your needs. Seek the Kingdom of God above all else, and live righteously, and he will give you everything you need (Matthew 6:26-33 NLT).

"Your heavenly Father already knows all your needs"— these are the words Jesus wants us to live by. When the enemy comes after us, saying, "Is that all the money you have in your bank account?" or "How on earth are you going to pay all that off?" stand in the truth of who God is and declare, "I see you, enemy, and I am not partnering with you. Today I am standing in my identity as a beloved child of God. Today I am partnering with Jehovah Jireh, the Lord Who Provides."

ABRAHAM'S STORY

In Genesis 22 we see this name of Jehovah Jireh first introduced. In the story of Abraham and Isaac, God gave Abraham an impossible task—go up to the mountain of the Lord and sacrifice his beloved son, Isaac. Now, keep in mind, Isaac was the promised son of Abraham. He had been birthed after Abraham was convinced his wife, Sarah, could no longer have children. In a way, Isaac was a miracle child and a gift from God.

Now, years before, when God had told Abraham he would be the "father of many nations," Abraham and Sarah believed this promise would come through their son, Isaac (Gen. 17:5 NLT). So, needless to say, sacrificing his son was a pretty hard command to follow. As Abraham walked Isaac up the mountain to certain death, he must have been questioning whether he had heard God correctly—either about the promise or the sacrifice. I can't imagine how much turmoil he must have gone through during this trek up the mountain.

Nevertheless, Abraham pushed through and followed the Lord's command. He took Isaac up the mountain, bound him, and raised his knife for the killing strike. But thankfully, God came through at the last moment and commanded him to stop. The Bible says:

> *And Abraham lifted up his eyes and looked, and behold, behind him was a ram, caught in a thicket by his horns. And Abraham went and took the ram and offered it up as a burnt offering instead of his son. So Abraham called the name of that place, "The Lord will provide"; as it is said to this day, "On the mount of the Lord it shall be provided"* (Genesis 22:13-14).

THE LORD, OUR PROVIDER

What would it look like if we actually believed Jehovah Jireh was in our midst? How would our lives change if we knew God's provision was available? I know in my own life, my attitude with finances would be different. I'd realize I was not alone with the bills, and the fear of not being able to pay them off would dissipate drastically.

In my own marriage with Stephen, I remember seasons in our early years when our finances taunted us. We'd feel our budgeted income was not equal to our expenses. And yet, somehow, God always managed to bring us through. Looking back at our early tax returns, we are reminded of the power of God's supernatural provision.

I love Pastor Bill Johnson's take on God's provision. In the passage where Jesus fed the five thousand, Bill points out that a spirit of poverty will always focus on what is lacking, whereas thankfulness celebrates what we currently have. In Matthew 14:13-21, when the disciples saw that the multitudes were hungry and asked Jesus to send them all home so they could eat, Jesus responded with, *"You give them something to eat"* (v. 16). Panicking, the disciples said, *"But we have here only five loaves of bread and two fish!"* (Matthew 14:17 NLT). Whereas Jesus was operating in faith, the disciples were partnering with a poverty spirit.

After the disciples reported their lack of provision, Jesus took the two fish and five loaves in His hands and gave thanks to God. Thankfulness ended up being the catalyst that invited God's Spirit to multiply the food. It provided a miraculous provision for the masses—teaching us that what little we do have is enough, because Jehovah Jireh is the God Who Provides.

What would it look like if we truly believed Jehovah Jireh was in our midst? How would we behave? Instead of focusing on lack and comparison, we could stand in our abundance and give thanks for what we do have.

In our own lives, practicing thankfulness might look like us paying off one bill out of ten and thanking God that we had the money to provide for that one in the first place. Or it might look like us taking ownership over our budgets and spending money only on the groceries we truly need. One time when I was going to the mailbox to send off a bill, I suddenly felt overwhelmed with joy about God's provision and began to dance around and laugh, even though I had several other bills I couldn't pay yet. Breakthrough did come, however, and eventually every bill was paid on time!

Reminding ourselves of who God is in the midst of our financial needs releases joy, because it reminds us of who God is. As we partner with His name, we stand in the midst of our situations in faith and declare, "I will not bow to fear of lack because Jehovah Jireh has everything I need."

OUR STORY

Years ago, when my husband and I were first starting out, we learned quickly about God's supernatural provision. In our early years, we had a situation where we did not receive a large sum of money we were expecting from an investment. At first, we were quite shocked and to be honest offended at the lack of honor shown to us. We went to dinner with our friend Faith Blatchford, who told us to write down the amount of money we felt we were owed and to present it to God. She said, "He will repay you for the money lost, but it won't come in the way you expect it."

Returning home, we wrote down the figure, $250,000, and said nothing else of our offense. About a week later, a young boy came up to Steve after the service and handed him a dollar. He told Steve that God had instructed him to give it to him. At that moment, we had an opportunity to be offended at the "little" God was providing us, or to rejoice in the small beginning to the breakthrough God was releasing. Instead, my husband said thank you and turned to me and said, "Someone is listening to God." As Stephen handed me the dollar, I felt God say, "Write it down. Keep track of My provision."

I began writing down every time we were given money or God's provision came through unexpectantly. I didn't write down what we earned—only the surprise money that came our way. Every time I wrote down a figure on the ledger, I thanked God for His provision. Within four years, our massive amount was paid in full. Praise Jesus! Jehovah Jireh was truly in our midst.

JEHOVAH SABAOTH

Another name of God I like to call upon is Jehovah Sabaoth, the Lord of Hosts. This is the name of God I call on when I am feeling like nothing is going my way—when I feel surrounded by my enemies, and when I need to be reminded that I am not alone.

Perhaps the most famous example of this in Scripture is found in Second Kings, the story of Elisha and his servant. In this story, the Persians, a hostile nation to the Israelites, surrounded the house of Elisha, God's prophet. Seeing the amassing armies, Elisha's servant panicked and said, *"Alas, my master! What shall we do?"*

Interestingly, Elisha did not partner with his servant's report. He instead, filled with faith, said, "Do not be afraid, for those who are with us are more than those who are with them." Here is the passage below:

> *And when the servant of the man of God arose early and went out, there was an army, surrounding the city with horses and chariots. And his servant said to him, "Alas, my master! What shall we do?" So he answered, "Do not fear, for those who are with us are more than those who are with them." And Elisha prayed, and said, "Lord, I pray, open his eyes that he may see." Then the Lord opened the eyes of the young man, and he saw. And behold, the mountain was full of horses and chariots of fire all around Elisha* (2 Kings 6:15-17 NKJV).

This story reminds me that no matter how dark my circumstances can be, God is still working on my behalf. When I am facing impossible situations, I get to turn to God and say, "Jehovah Sabaoth, please reveal to me Your hosts that are protecting me and fighting for me in this situation."

CALLING ON THE LORD OF HOSTS

In my own life, I have had to learn the importance of partnering with this aspect of God. Perhaps the moment I felt this the most was when I was working for a small Christian school in Redding, California, as an accountant. During a very difficult financial season for the school, governmental programs in our community were being implemented and putting a strain on our finances. Student enrollment was falling, and it seemed to be getting worse every day.

As the finance manager, I was struggling daily to see God's provision. I came into my office every morning and said, "God, we need You to come through," yet I still didn't see Him changing our stressful financial situation. Then finally, in what felt like a last straw, one of our student's homes burned to the ground, and the youngest daughter of the family passed away in the flames. The sudden tragedy was so heartbreaking that we found ourselves in shock in an already stressful situation. I remember all the teachers gathering together in the student lounge and saying, "What are we going to do?"

We were fed up with the enemy's attacks but had no idea how to react. We felt that not only had the wind been taken out of our sails, but we were on our last legs. Standing together in prayer, we simply said, "God, where are You? And what are You going to do?" In the midst of all this pain, I remember saying, "God, if You don't show up, I don't think our school is going to make it."

I was literally calling upon the name of Jehovah Sabaoth to release His angels to do battle for us. To this day, I am still not sure exactly how we made it through that season as a faculty. In a way, we sort of just numbly walked along through it. What I do remember is at some point the attacks against us seemed to quiet down and eventually we turned the corner. Somehow we made it through and not only did our school survive, but we came together as a solid unit and upheld the family who had lost their child. I believe this was because Jehovah Sabaoth, the Lord of Hosts, was doing battle for us. When you are battle-fatigued, invite Jehovah Sabaoth to send His army to do battle for you.

ELI AND HANNAH'S STORY

One of my favorite stories in Scripture showing the power of the Lord of Hosts is the exchange between Eli, God's prophet, and Hannah, the future mother of Samuel. Heartbroken at not being able to provide a son for her husband, Hannah went to the temple to pray, and she did so with such ferocity that the head priest, Eli, thought she was drunk.

In the midst of her grief, the Lord of Hosts heard Hannah's complaints and granted her request. This passage shows me that even in the midst of our impossible situations, we can turn to the Lord of Hosts and ask for His blessing to come and invade our situation. Here is the passage below:

After they had eaten and drunk in Shiloh, Hannah rose. Now Eli the priest was sitting on the seat beside the doorpost of the temple of the Lord. She was deeply distressed and prayed to the Lord and wept bitterly. And she vowed a vow and said, "O Lord of Hosts, if you will indeed look on the affliction of your servant and remember me and not forget your servant, but will give to your servant a son, then I will give him to the Lord all the days of his life, and no razor shall touch his head." As she continued praying before the Lord, Eli observed her mouth. Hannah was speaking in her heart; only her lips moved, and her voice was not heard. Therefore Eli took her to be a drunken woman. And Eli said to her, "How long will you go on being drunk? Put your wine away from you." But Hannah answered, "No, my lord, I am a woman troubled in spirit. I have drunk neither wine nor strong drink, but I have been pouring out my soul before the Lord. Do not regard your servant as a worthless woman, for all along I have been speaking out of my great anxiety and vexation." Then Eli answered, "Go in peace, and the God of Israel grant your petition that you have made to him" (1 Samuel 1:9-17).

Due to God's grace, Hannah gave birth to Samuel, her miraculous child, who later became the prophet who anointed David as king. I love this story because it shows me how crying out to God and being on my last leg can truly lead to radical breakthrough.

When we are feeling overwhelmed and alone in our struggles, we must remember that the Lord of Hosts is fighting for us. We may need to refresh our vision through prayer like in Second Kings with Elisha and his servant. When we find ourselves in overwhelming seasons, asking God to open our eyes to see His armies rallying around us is the best way to overcome our struggles. As we wait to see what the Lord reveals, we must keep in mind that whatever issues we are facing might be physical, provisional, or spiritual. It is important to take notice of how we feel in these situations. If we feel lost and abandoned and cannot stand one more moment in the heat of battle, this is the prayer we must release. The Bible says:

> *Therefore put on the full armor of God, so that when the day of evil comes, you may be able to stand your ground, and after you have done everything, to stand* (Ephesians 6:13 NIV).

When you find yourself in the middle of a fight and feel completely surrounded, plant yourself firmly in God's Word and realize the importance of standing with God in the midst of your fight. If your arms feel tired from carrying weapons, ask for the angelic realm to bring reinforcements. Say, "Not today, enemy. I cast you out of my life. The Lord of Hosts is at my side."

If you feel tired and alone in the midst of battle, break off any attachments you may have with fear. Forgive anyone who has abandoned you in the past. Rebuke any lies that are saying you are alone and that your spiritual battle is bigger than the Lord's ability to invade the situation. When you feel this way, call on Jehovah Sabaoth, the Lord of Hosts. Consider these verses:

> *He who dwells in the shelter of the Most High will abide in the shadow of the Almighty. I will say to the Lord, "My refuge and my fortress, my God, in whom I trust."...A thousand may fall at your side, ten thousand at your right hand, but it will not come near you* (Psalm 91:1-2,7).

As you ponder the words of this passage and go throughout your day, ask yourself, "What am I trusting in?" Are you believing in your own strength? Or your bank account? Or are you trusting in the all-powerful, loving God?

Sometimes when you are discouraged, it is hard to keep moving forward. You may stop and think, "I don't know what to do, so I'll just wait until I get some direction from God." Although this might work in some seasons, I have found most of the time God wants us to keep moving forward. As we move, He partners with us and keeps us on the path toward victory. As we step out in faith, God brings reinforcements.

If you are already moving forward but still feel assaulted, declare over yourself that you are stepping into a Psalm 91 season. This means you are positioning yourself in the shadow of the Almighty's wings. God will deliver you from the snare and the deadly pestilence.

I declare that the Lord of Hosts is with You and that He sends His hosts wherever you feel overwhelmed. I declare that the lies that have been discouraging you are going to be silenced and cut off in Jesus's name. Take a moment right now and meditate on Psalm 91 and ask the Holy Spirit to give you a deeper revelation as you read:

> *He who dwells in the shelter of the Most High will abide in the shadow of the Almighty. I will say to the Lord, "My refuge and my fortress, my God, in whom I trust." For he will deliver you from the snare of the fowler and from the deadly pestilence. He will cover you with his pinions, and under his wings you will find refuge; his faithfulness is a shield and buckler. You will not fear the terror of the night, nor the arrow that flies by day, nor the pestilence that stalks in darkness, nor the destruction that wastes at noonday. A thousand may fall at your side, ten thousand at your right hand, but it will not come near you. You will only look with your eyes and see the recompense of the wicked. Because you have made the Lord your dwelling place— the Most High, who is my refuge— no evil shall be allowed to befall you, no plague come near your tent. For he will command his angels concerning you to guard you in all your ways. On their hands they will bear you up, lest you strike your foot against a*

stone. You will tread on the lion and the adder; the young lion and the serpent you will trample underfoot. "Because he holds fast to me in love, I will deliver him; I will protect him, because he knows my name. When he calls to me, I will answer him; I will be with him in trouble; I will rescue him and honor him. With long life I will satisfy him and show him my salvation."

Read through Psalm 91 anytime you need Jehovah Sabaoth and invite Him to send His hosts as reinforcements into your situation, and tuck up under His wings. Every time you read these verses, let the words speak truth into your spirit and conform your mind to His. Jehovah Sabaoth is with you always. He is your help and will send reinforcements as you need.

SUMMARY

POINT TO PONDER

God is our provider and protector. It is in His nature to provide for us in our times of need.

VERSE TO REMEMBER

And my God will supply all your needs according to His riches in glory in Christ Jesus.
—PHILIPPIANS 4:19 NASB

QUESTIONS TO CONSIDER

1. Are you feeling overwhelmed by any difficult financial situations?

2. Have you found yourself in a pattern of grumbling about your situations instead of being thankful?

3. Do you feel like there is absolutely no way for you to get out of the current situations you are in?

PRAYER

Thank You, Jesus, for being my provider and protector. I hand to You all my needs of shelter and provision. I ask that You keep me in the shadow of Your wings. Protect me as I move forward into the dreams You have called me to pursue. Fill my life with Your blessing and help me to stay thankful.

ACTIVATION

Take a bill or financial milestone you are having difficulty paying off. As a prophetic act, place it beneath your feet and ask Jehovah Jireh, the Lord Who Provides, to step into the midst of your situation. Declare that His blessing is enough, and ask for practical steps, if necessary, you can take to see this mountain fall. Believe your need will be taken care of and watch as the Lord brings provision.

CHAPTER 9

HIS NAME, HIS NATURE (PART III)

*Nathanael said to Him, "How do **you** know me?" Jesus answered and said to him, "Before Philip called **you**, when **you** were under the fig tree, **I saw you**."*
—JOHN 1:48 NKJV

Jehovah Roi, the God Who Sees, is another name of God I use often in battle. In fact, it is one of the most important names for us to remember. I say this because if we understand that God actually sees us and our situations, many of the devil's attacks on our lives would be ineffective.

We wouldn't be afraid of the enemy's attacks because we'd know God already sees our situation. Even in moments where we feel caught unaware, we'd know He is watching us and is not surprised by the enemy's attacks. Sickness, financial struggles, and relational troubles wouldn't seem impossible to overcome. We'd know God has a plan for us to step out of it.

When we know that God is the One who sees, we realize every situation we will ever face is winnable. We understand that because our situations don't catch God unaware, Jehovah Roi, the God Who Sees, already has a plan of escape for us.

THE GOD WHO SEES

I love the story in Scripture where this name of God is first mentioned. Jehovah Roi appears in the story of Hagar, Sarai's servant, and her son, Ishmael.

For those who are not familiar with this story, it centers around God's promise to Abram that he would be the father of many nations. This was a radical word at the time because Abram was nearly a hundred years old and Sarai, his wife, was barren.

Feeling devalued at not being able to provide her husband a child, Sarai decided to take matters into her own hands. She convinced Abram to have relations with her servant, Hagar, who became pregnant with Abram's son, Ishmael. Scripture says:

Now Sarai, Abram's wife, had not been able to bear children for him. But she had an Egyptian servant named Hagar. So Sarai said to Abram, "The Lord has prevented me from having children. Go and sleep with my servant. Perhaps I can have children through her." And Abram agreed with Sarai's proposal. So Sarai, Abram's wife, took Hagar the Egyptian servant and gave her to Abram as a wife. (This happened ten years after Abram had settled in the land of Canaan.) So Abram had sexual relations with Hagar, and she became pregnant. But when Hagar knew she was pregnant, she began to treat her mistress, Sarai, with contempt (Genesis 16:1-4 NLT).

For whatever reason, Hagar began to view Sarai with contempt. Maybe it was jealousy or envy. Either way, Sarai, unable to handle the tension, went to her husband in rage and demanded her servant be cast out. The Bible says:

Then Sarai said to Abram, "This is all your fault! I put my servant into your arms, but now that she's pregnant she treats me with contempt. The Lord will show who's wrong—you or me!" Abram replied, "Look, she is your servant, so deal with her as you see fit." Then Sarai treated Hagar so harshly that she finally ran away (Genesis 16:5-6 NLT).

This story is so interesting because it shows how caring God is in the midst of our troubles. Abram and Sarai were

God's chosen people; Hagar was just their servant. Yet once Hagar fled and got lost in the desert, she was visited by an angel of the Lord and given assurance that she would be protected. Here is the passage below:

> *The angel of the Lord found her* [Hagar] *by a spring of water in the wilderness, the spring on the way to Shur. And he said, "Hagar, servant of Sarai, where have you come from and where are you going?" She said, "I am fleeing from my mistress Sarai." The angel of the Lord said to her, "Return to your mistress and submit to her"* (Genesis 16:7-9).

I love this story because it doesn't center around someone who was perfect. Hagar was in rebellion and was running away from a messy situation, yet God still met her in the midst of her rebellion and gave her a promise of protection. Here is the verse below:

> *And the angel also said, "You are now pregnant and will give birth to a son. You are to name him Ishmael (which means 'God hears'), for the Lord has heard your cry of distress"* (Genesis 16:11 NLT).

This passage encourages me that in times when I feel like I might have failed, I can still know God sees me, loves me, and wants to come through and rescue me. Like Hagar, I can rest in the assurance that I am seen and loved by God, even when I may be acting inappropriately.

At the end of this story, Hagar named the place God visited her Beer-lahai-roi, "the well of the Living One who sees me" and returned to Sarai. Amazed at the goodness of God, Hagar returned home feeling loved and full of hope. Consider this verse:

> *Thereafter, Hagar used another name to refer to the Lord, who had spoken to her. She said, "You are the God Who Sees me." She also said, "Have I truly seen the One who sees me?" So that well was named Beer-lahai-roi (which means "well of the Living One who sees me"). It can still be found between Kadesh and Bered* (Genesis 16:13-14 NLT).

WHEN GOD SEES

Sometimes I think that when we don't believe God sees us, partnering with sin becomes easy. We think, "God's not really watching, so I can have this extra drink." Or "He's not seeing me when I fudge on my taxes, so He's not really seeing my sin." Sin becomes easy when we don't believe the Lord sees, but the other side of the coin is condemnation, which the enemy can also use to harass us.

The truth is when we welcome Jehovah Roi, the God Who Sees, into our midst, the result is freedom. Freedom is a gift God gives us when we stand in the reality that He sees us and protects us even in the midst of our sin. Even when we are trapped in our lowest points, God has mercy on us.

To see more of God's kindness in the midst of our sin, consider this story of the Samaritan woman at the well:

> *Jesus said to her, "Go, call your husband, and come here." The woman answered and said, "I have no husband." Jesus said to her, "You have well said, 'I have no husband,' for you have had five husbands, and the one whom you now have is not your husband; in that you spoke truly."... The woman said to Him, "I know that Messiah is coming" (who is called Christ). "When He comes, He will tell us all things." Jesus said to her, "I who speak to you am He." And at this point His disciples came, and they marveled that He talked with a woman; yet no one said, "What do You seek?" or, "Why are You talking with her?" The woman then left her waterpot, went her way into the city, and said to the men, "Come, see a Man who told me all things that I ever did. Could this be the Christ?" Then they went out of the city and came to Him....And many of the Samaritans of that city believed in Him because of the word of the woman who testified, "He told me all that I ever did" (John 4:16-18, 25-30, 39 NKJV).*

In this story, Jesus saw the Samaritan woman in the midst of her sin and loved her. He didn't send her away in shame or condemnation but welcomed her with love. This demonstration of grace led to the woman's freedom and ultimately the salvation of her entire city.

The enemy is always trying to pervert the true nature of God. He tells us, "You can't trust Him. He won't forgive you. God's angry. He'll punish you." Although God is the judge and He has no place for sin, He is still rich and bountiful with love. If we have a repentant heart and are willing to renounce our sins and call upon the name of Jesus, freedom is the inevitable result. Consider these verses:

> *The Lord is merciful and compassionate, slow to get angry and filled with unfailing love....He showers compassion on all his creation* (Psalm 145:8-9 NLT).

Not only is it good to remember God's compassion but also to realize He sees all. When I am going through hard situations, I remind myself that my circumstances did not catch God unaware. He still sees me—no matter how lost or abandoned I feel. This declaration encourages me often in these times: You know what, God, I bet You saw this coming, and because You saw it coming, I bet You have a way of escape for me.

Sometimes I think the real issue is that we feel God is not paying attention to us. We think God has left us to fend for ourselves, but this is not true. No matter how alone and unseen we feel, we are never out of God's sight. Consider this passage:

Where can I go from your Spirit? Or where can I flee from your presence? If I ascend to heaven, You are there; If I make my bed in Sheol, behold, You are there. If I take the wings of the dawn, If I dwell in the remotest part of the sea, Even there Your hand will guide me, And Your right hand will lay hold of me (Psalm 139:7-10 NASB).

When you can't see God, it's important to remember He is right there with you. He has always been there, and even in those times when you don't feel Him, He sees you. God sees what you have been struggling with and is happy to help you out of any mess you have gotten yourself into. No matter what season you are in or how depressed you may feel, God sees your situation. It is impossible for you to outrun or hide or be abandoned from the One Who Sees.

JEHOVAH SHALOM

Peace I leave with you; my peace I give you. I do not give to you as the world gives. Do not let your hearts be troubled and do not be afraid (John 14:27 NIV).

The final name I want to cover is Jehovah Shalom, the God of Peace. This is the name I turn to when I am feeling stressed, overwhelmed, or afraid of life's circumstances. In these seasons, I turn to Jehovah Shalom, the God of Peace, and invite His presence to come in and change my perspective.

The first time Jehovah Shalom appears in Scripture is the story of Gideon. Here is the full passage below:

Now the angel of the Lord came and sat under the terebinth at Ophrah, which belonged to Joash the Abiezrite, while his son Gideon was beating out wheat in the winepress to hide it from the Midianites. And the angel of the Lord appeared to him and said to him, "The Lord is with you, O mighty man of valor." And Gideon said to him, "Please, my lord, if the Lord is with us, why then has all this happened to us? And where are all his wonderful deeds that our fathers recounted to us, saying, 'Did not the Lord bring us up from Egypt?' But now the Lord has forsaken us and given us into the hand of Midian." And the Lord turned to him and said, "Go in this might of yours and save Israel from the hand of Midian; do not I send you?" And he said to him, "Please, Lord, how can I save Israel? Behold, my clan is the weakest in Manasseh, and I am the least in my father's house." And the Lord said to him, "But I will be with you, and you shall strike the Midianites as one man." And he said to him, "If now I have found favor in your eyes, then show me a sign that it is you who speak with me. Please do not depart from here until I come to you and bring out my present and set it before you." And he said, "I will stay till you return."

So Gideon went into his house and prepared a young goat and unleavened cakes from an ephah of flour. The meat he put in a basket, and the broth he put in a pot, and brought them to him under the terebinth and presented them. And the angel of God said to him, "Take the meat and the unleavened cakes, and put them on this rock, and pour the broth over them." And he did so. Then the angel of the Lord reached out the tip of the staff that was in his hand and touched the meat and the unleavened cakes. And fire sprang up from the rock and consumed the meat and the unleavened cakes. And the angel of the Lord vanished from his sight. Then Gideon perceived that he was the angel of the Lord. And Gideon said, "Alas, O Lord God! For now I have seen the angel of the Lord face to face." But the Lord said to him, "Peace be to you. Do not fear; you shall not die." Then Gideon built an altar there to the Lord and called it, The Lord Is Peace. To this day it still stands at Ophrah, which belongs to the Abiezrites (Judges 6:11-24).

To get the full benefit of this story, we need to understand its context. During this time in Israel's history, the Midianites were running continual raids, slaughtering the Israelites, and confiscating their crops. Gideon, a member of Israel's smallest tribe, was so scared of being attacked that he hid in a winepress while he was threshing wheat.

Needless to say, Gideon's circumstances were far from peaceful, yet this is exactly where the Lord found him.

When the angel of the Lord appeared, he called Gideon a "mighty man of valor." Right off, the angel cut through all the negative thoughts Gideon had about himself. Gideon believed he was abandoned by God and had a hard time believing the Lord's words. When Gideon heard the Lord's encouragement, his first response was "If God is with us, then why is all this bad stuff happening?"

I too can identify with Gideon's statement. Many times clients I work with feel abandoned and ignored by God. Until they can reject the enemy's voice and accept God's truth, they have a hard time believing what He wants to tell them.

The enemy's number-one weapon he uses against us is fear, and fear always comes when we believe the devil's lies. This is why it is important for us to always renounce the devil's falsehoods and conform to God's truth. When we align our minds with Christ's, lies and fear evaporate. This is how we learn to connect to God's peace.

What I think is interesting about Gideon's story is the angel of the Lord did not respond directly to Gideon's complaints. He instead said, *"But I will be with you, and you shall strike the Midianites as one man"* (v. 16).

Even with this statement, Gideon was not completely assured. He had been so badly beaten down by his adversaries that he continued to test the angel's proclamations by asking God to give him miraculous signs. When the last sign was fulfilled by God, Gideon fell down upon his face in awe because he finally realized he truly was in the presence of the Almighty God. Gideon said, *"Alas, O Lord God! For now I have seen the angel of the Lord face to face"* (v. 22). Instead of rebuking Gideon, the angel said, *"Peace be to you. Do not fear; you shall not die"* (v. 23).

After this exchange, Gideon built an altar to the Lord and called it The Lord Is Peace, showing his thankfulness for encountering the God who brought peace into his situation.

As Christians, we need to realize we have access to this peace. The natural peace the world tries to conjure up rarely ever works. False ideas of submission and zero conflict only lead to further stress down the road. The true kind of peace, the kind that lasts, comes only from God.

Thankfully, we have access to this peace because we serve Jehovah Shalom, the God of Peace, and we can receive His peace through our connection with Jesus, our righteousness. When we don't feel God's peace, it means we need to realign ourselves with Jehovah Shalom and ask for His peace that passes understanding (see Phil. 4:7). Whenever we feel attacked or discouraged in life, we need to remember it is the God of Peace that crushes satan under His feet (see Rom. 16:20).

Take some time right now and think about the Midianites that are attacking your life. It could be your job, your friends, or your finances. Maybe it is a spiritual, emotional, or physical attack. Or maybe there is a specific type of demonic spirit that is trying to steal your peace.

Once you identify whatever is harassing you, declare into the atmosphere, "I see you [insert whatever it is the Lord shows you]. You are going down in Jesus's name. Jehovah Shalom, release Your peace into my life and shift the atmospheres around me to peace so I can be reseated with You in the heavenlies."

CONCLUSION

One last comment before we close. Partnering with Jehovah Shalom, the God of Peace, does not mean everything in your life will be easy. However, you will be able to rest in the midst of the storm. If you feel you have been oppressed, exhausted, worn down, or kicked around because of fear or invading circumstances, say, "Jehovah Shalom, I hand You the lie that You have not been paying attention to my situation. I say to the spirits that have been harassing me, you need to come stand next to my God, Jehovah Shalom, the God of Peace. I am not invisible to my God, Jehovah Roi, and I say to these Midianites in my life—I see you. I am not partnering with you anymore, and I command you to depart in Jesus's name. Amen."

If you feel unsettled after repeating this prayer, say, "Jesus, are You going to take care of me as I step out of hiding and work to fulfill Your commands? Father God, I repent for believing the lie that You have overlooked me.

I declare my life is going to be drastically changed. I am recalibrating the truth today that You see me and that You protect me. I say to my circumstances, 'You don't stand a chance against my God.' Amen."

Ask the Lord for wisdom on how to move forward through any circumstances you are currently facing. Ask Him if there is a lie you are believing that is empowering fear in the midst of your situation. If the Lord identifies a lie, ask Him where you learned it (Was it during childhood? Who taught it to you?). Forgive anyone who taught you this lie and hand it to Jesus and ask what truth He wants to put in its place. When you receive this truth, ask Him how you can activate it in a practical way.

Take a moment now and declare this revelation over your life: "I see you, enemy, and today you are under my feet." This is a prophetic declaration telling your spirit and the atmosphere around you that your life and circumstances are under your feet. Say to the enemy, "The God of Peace is crushing you [insert here whatever is trying to steal your peace] under my feet," and stomp on the enemy in a prophetic activation of truth.

In spiritual warfare, you must use God's truths to combat the enemy. When the devil tries to tell you God is small and he is big, remind yourself of God's power and ability to get you through. Practice reminding yourself daily that it is the God of Peace and not satan who has everything under control.

Summary

Points to Ponder

God sees you in every situation. He knows what you are facing, and He has prepared you for it.

Verse to Remember

Grace and peace be yours in abundance through the knowledge of God and of Jesus our Lord.
—2 Peter 1:2 NIV

Questions to Consider:

1. Do you feel like God has forgotten you?

2. Are you in a situation you did not expect?

3. Do you feel overwhelmed by life's circumstances?

4. Do you know how to carry peace into the midst of life's storms?

PRAYER

Thank You, Jesus, that You see me in every season of life. I renounce the lie that I am forgotten and abandoned. Thank You that You see this season I am in and You have already provided a way out for me. Protect me as I move forward in this area and seek Your resolution.

ACTIVATION

Write down any areas of your life where you don't feel seen. This could be in your house, at your job, or in your marriage. Offer these areas to God and ask Him for the truth that He wants You to know. After you hear His truths, write them down in each area and declare His peace over your situations.

CHAPTER 10

SLAYING GOLIATHS

*Then David said to the Philistine [Goliath],
"You come to me with a sword and with a spear
and with a javelin, but I come to you in the
name of the Lord of Hosts, the God of the armies
of Israel, whom you have defied. This day the
Lord will deliver you into my hand, and I will
strike you down and cut off your head. And
I will give the dead bodies of the host of the
Philistines this day to the birds of the air and
to the wild beasts of the earth, that all the earth
may know that there is a God in Israel, and that
all this assembly may know that the Lord saves
not with sword and spear. For the battle is the
Lord's, and he will give you into our hand."*

—1 Samuel 17:45-47

To be victorious in spiritual warfare, we need to learn how to face off against the Goliaths that are harassing us. Goliaths are scary situations, powerful demonic spirits, or other obstacles that are trying to cause fear in our lives. Some examples of Goliaths can be a loved one receiving a cancer diagnosis, someone having to work with a tormenting boss, or an individual facing impending financial ruin. As Christians, we need to learn how to disarm these Goliaths and partner with God's hope and everlasting peace.

THE POWER OF TESTIMONIES

At my church, we live in a testimony culture. We meditate daily on the testimonies of what God has done in the past. We believe this shows the nature of our God and encourages us to believe His nature will remain true in our current situations. This helps us to live with expectancy of what God is going to do in our trials and tribulations. When an obstacle rears its ugly head, we believe God's goodness will overcome it.

Testimonies are powerful tools we can use because it gives us a weapon that grants us access to faith. The Bible says the testimony of Jesus is the spirit of prophecy (see Rev. 19:10). Whenever we speak God's testimonies into the atmosphere, we release hope and steward an expectancy that He will once again pull us through our struggles.

Testimonies serve the same purpose as memorial stones from Scripture. They remind us of what God can do. Consider this passage from Joshua:

When all the nation had finished passing over the Jordan, the Lord said to Joshua, "Take twelve men from the people, from each tribe a man, and command them, saying, 'Take twelve stones from here out of the midst of the Jordan, from the very place where the priests' feet stood firmly, and bring them over with you and lay them down in the place where you lodge tonight.'" Then Joshua called the twelve men from the people of Israel, whom he had appointed, a man from each tribe. And Joshua said to them, "Pass on before the ark of the Lord your God into the midst of the Jordan, and take up each of you a stone upon his shoulder, according to the number of the tribes of the people of Israel, that this may be a sign among you. When your children ask in time to come, 'What do those stones mean to you?' then you shall tell them that the waters of the Jordan were cut off before the ark of the covenant of the Lord. When it passed over the Jordan, the waters of the Jordan were cut off. So these stones shall be to the people of Israel a memorial forever" (Joshua 4:1-7).

In this passage, the Israelites' stones served as memorials that reminded the people of what God had done. When future generations would stop and ask their parents what these stones could mean, the older generations could recount God's miraculous blessings and encourage them that the Lord who did this breakthrough in the past could do it again.

Our testimonies serve the same purpose as these price-less memorial stones. They point us to the breakthroughs God has done in the past and direct us to the possibilities of what God can do in the future. When we tell others or remind ourselves of what God has already done, it reminds us of His nature and encourages us that His goodness can shine through into our current situations. When we hear about people receiving salvation, we are reminded of Jehovah Tsidkenu, the God Our Righteousness (see Jer. 23:5-6). When we hear about God's provision, we are reminded of Jehovah Jireh, the Lord Who Provides (see Gen. 22:1-14). When we hear testimonies of people being healed, it reminds us of Jehovah Rapha, the God Who Heals.

The enemy is always trying to taunt us by masquerading himself as too big for God's goodness to overcome. When we are facing the enemy in the form of sickness or disease, a difficult marriage, or a poor job situation, it is impor-tant to remember the memorial stones God has placed in our lives. When we are feeling surrounded by the enemy's attacks, we need to remember what God has already done and be thankful that His goodness has not changed.

DAVID, THE GIANT KILLER

In First Samuel 17 the Bible shares the famous story of David and Goliath. As one of the most recognizable passages in Scripture, it gives us a look at someone who was fearless in the face of danger and partnered with God to destroy a seemingly indestructible enemy. When the armies of Israel were frightened and refused to accept Goliath's challenge to face him in battle, David became the sole person willing to do so.

In our own lives, we can learn a lot from David. We may initially think of him standing before Goliath as the great king surrounded by his mighty men, but this was years before he had even assembled his band of heroes. In this story, David was not yet a great warrior. Rather he was a young shepherd filled with great courage, who, while protecting his father's sheep in the past, managed to kill a lion and a bear.

These experiences with God—the victories over the lion and the bear—were David's memorial stones—his testimonies. So when Goliath stood out in defiance against the armies of Israel, David did not hesitate to believe God would come through once again and save him. With God's help, David had already killed a lion and a bear with his bare hands, so he knew in his heart that facing this giant would lead to victory. Consider this passage:

> [Goliath] *stood and shouted to the ranks of Israel and said to them, "Why do you come out to draw up in battle array? Am I not the Philistine and you servants of Saul? Choose a man for yourselves and let him come down to me. If he is able to fight with me and kill me, then we will become your servants; but if I prevail against him and kill him, then you shall become our servants and serve us." Again the Philistine said, "I defy the*

ranks of Israel this day; give me a man that we may fight together."...As he [David] *was talking with* [his brothers], *behold, the champion, the Philistine from Gath named Goliath, was coming up from the army of the Philistines, and he spoke these same words; and David heard them* (1 Samuel 17:8-10, 23 NASB).

It is important to note that Goliath's taunt in this passage was not the first time he had called out to the armies of Israel. It was simply the first time David had heard it. Other verses show us the Philistines and Israelites had been lining up against each other every morning, but because Goliath was so big and the armies of Israel were so afraid, no one had yet accepted the giant's challenge.

In our own lives, we have Goliaths that we face on a daily basis. We get up every day hoping our lives will be different only to run into the same problems once again. When it comes to us facing these giants, our response must be to not cower in fear but rather to align ourselves with God who has defeated our enemies before.

In David's example, his reaction was outrage at hearing his enemy mock God. Taking Goliath's insults personally, David asked his fellow soldiers, *"Who is this uncircumcised Philistine, that he should defy the armies of the living God?"* (v. 26). David wasn't fighting Goliath for his own name but for God's, and this became the fuel that urged him to victory.

In our own lives, we need to remember that our Goliaths are not just problems we are facing. They are problems trying to defy the very nature of our God: our God the healer, our God the provider, and our God of Peace. When facing life's Goliaths, we need to lean into the nature of God that we have already seen established in our lives and pull on these testimonies as a source of strength. This can lead us to righteous anger (like it did with David), an overwhelming sense of peace (like with Jesus in the storm), or even a joyful determination (like with Jesus when He endured the cross). However God's testimonies inspire us, we need to pull on them and use them as fuel to propel us forward through the fight.

SAUL QUESTIONS DAVID

Interestingly, David's fervent faith did not elicit cheering but mocking. His older brothers told him to keep quiet. But somehow King Saul heard of David's courage and brought him forward to see if he would be able to take on the Philistine's challenge. When Saul asked David if he had even fought in battles before, David said:

> *"Your servant used to keep his father's sheep, and when a lion or a bear came and took a lamb out of the flock, I went out after it and struck it, and delivered the lamb from its mouth; and when it arose against me, I caught it by its beard, and struck and killed it. Your servant has killed both lion and bear; and this uncircumcised Philistine will be like one of them, seeing he has defied the armies of the living God." Moreover David said,*

"The Lord, who delivered me from the paw of the lion and from the paw of the bear, He will deliver me from the hand of this Philistine" (1 Samuel 17:34-37 NKJV).

David couldn't tell Saul he had killed a giant before because he hadn't. But instead of bowing to intimidation, David told Saul of his exploits while tending his father's sheep. He used the testimonies of what God had already done in the past to show that once again he would emerge victorious.

In David's case, he had never killed a giant, but he had killed a lion and a bear. Because of God's nature as a rescuer and a deliverer, David knew Goliath would also be defeated.

In your own life, you may not have fought the specific Goliaths that are rearing their heads against you, but you have fought and overcome other attacks from the enemy that once tried to take you out. Looking at your own life, ask yourself, "Have I fought a lion? Have I fought a bear?" Maybe you are facing cancer. You have not seen this sickness bow before, but maybe you have prayed for someone who was suffering from migraines and they were healed. If so, that is your lion. Hold onto it and receive it as a victory from God, and realize He will grant you victory again.

USING YOUR OWN SKILLS

In David's story with Goliath, we see an interesting exchange where Saul tries to clothe David in his own armor. Obviously, the armor doesn't fit and David ends up choosing his normal shepherd's cloak. Consider this passage from Scripture:

> *Then Saul clothed David with his armor. He put a helmet of bronze on his head and clothed him with a coat of mail, and David strapped his sword over his armor. And he tried in vain to go, for he had not tested them. Then David said to Saul, "I cannot go with these, for I have not tested them." So David put them off. Then he took his staff from his hand and chose five smooth stones from the brook and put them in his shepherd's pouch. His sling was in his hand, and he approached the Philistine* (1 Samuel 17:38-40).

In this passage, Saul was trying to put his own armor on David (his own personal testimonies). Normally, this would be a good idea, but in this case, it didn't work. When we are facing giants, it is helpful to pull on the testimonies of others, but in this battle, David knew he needed to wield his own testimonies to defeat this Goliath.

In your life, be sure to spend time with God so you can identify which season you are in. Sometimes you will need to partner with someone else's testimonies to increase your faith. In others, you will need to encourage yourself against a new foe with your own testimonies of what God has already done specifically for you.

Notice that David's response to Saul's command was, *"I cannot go with these, for I have not tested them."* Sometimes when we gird ourselves with the testimonies of others, the enemy tries to wear us down and destroy our faith. He whispers lies like, "Sure, God healed that lady, but He won't heal you" or "That person is so much more righteous than you, so of course they received their breakthrough." When the enemy is taunting you in this way, pull out your own testimonies—even when they seem small in comparison to what you are facing. Test your testimonies against the enemy and see what the Lord is willing to do. Once you have successfully tested your testimonies against satan and have emerged victorious, there is nothing the enemy can do to talk you out of truth!

Summary

Points to Ponder

When the enemy is taunting you in the midst of battle, testimonies of what God has done for others can be memorial stones that point you to the nature of God. If this doesn't bring you the courage you need, ask God to show you what your own testimonies of victory are and hurl those at the enemy.

Verse to Remember

Then I fell down at his feet to worship him, but he said to me, "You must not do that! I am a fellow servant with you and your brothers who hold to the testimony of Jesus. Worship God." For the testimony of Jesus is the spirit of prophecy.
—Revelations 19:10

QUESTIONS TO CONSIDER

1. What testimonies do you already have in your life that show God coming through for you?

2. Are you currently facing a Goliath that is tormenting you?

3 Can you recall anyone you know that has beaten a similar giant before?

4. What lies are you hearing from the enemy regarding your situation?

PRAYER

Thank You, Jesus, for the power of Your testimonies. I release breakthrough over my life and command every giant I am facing to fall. In Your holy name, dispatch Heaven's angels of warfare and remove any and all ungodly mountains from my life.

ACTIVATION

Take out a piece of paper and make two lists. For the first list, write the label "Breakthrough Needed." Ask God what He wants you to put on this list. (Note: these may be personal, related to family or business, or even some overall need for your country.) After praying this, write down whatever needs God reveals. When you are finished, turn your paper over or create a new list and label this "My Testimonies."

Now ask God to show you answered prayers and testimonies in your life. Write them down as He reveals them. (Note: these testimonies can be as small as "I prayed for someone whose back was hurting and it was healed" or as big as "I received a million dollar check in the mail!")

If, while you are praying you don't feel like you have a testimony, ask yourself, "Am I saved?" (If you have made it this far in the book then you probably are.) If being saved is the only testimony that comes to mind, then write it down and celebrate with Jesus, because that is the greatest testimony you will ever receive! If you happen to not yet know the King of kings, then take a moment right now and invite Jesus into your heart. Wise warriors are always those who partner with Jesus.

One of my friends who did this exercise asked the Holy Spirit, "Holy Spirit, what is a testimony I have?" Instantly she heard, "You are still alive. In your crazy family, you wouldn't have made it to today without Me." So she wrote down, "I'm still alive" and rejoiced.

As you ponder the testimonies God has shared with you, go back to your "Breakthroughs Needed" list and ask Him to show you any other giants that are present in your life. Write these down.

Now, reread your testimonies out loud. These are your defeated lions and bears. These are the breakthroughs God has already given to you. Thank God for what He has already done and position yourself for the faith that He is about to do something new.

Turn back to the "Breakthroughs Needed" list and say, "Needs, do you see this list of testimonies? I declare you will be made like them in Jesus's name! You will no longer terrify me. My God is so much bigger than you."

Continue to write down other victories you have experienced with God throughout your week. Then every time the enemy raises his head to taunt you, put these testimonies in your hands and shake them at him.

Remember, the enemy is not just harassing you; he is trying to defy the nature of the living God.

ABOUT DAWNA DE SILVA

Dawna De Silva is the founder and coleader with Teresa Liebscher of Bethel Sozo International ministry. She and her husband, Stephen De Silva, have been ministering from Bethel for the past twenty years as well as preaching, speaking, and authoring books. Dawna's manual on shifting atmospheres has become a sought-after tool for daily empowerment. Whether training Sozo, preaching, shifting atmospheres, or ministering prophetically, Dawna releases people, churches, and cities into new vision and freedom. No matter how traumatic the wounding, Dawna ministers with authority and gentleness, imparting hope and healing. You can follow Dawna on Twitter, Facebook, or her own personal website at www.dawnadesilva.com. Please send any testimonies you have about warring wisely to Dawna at dawna.desilva@bethel.com.

More Books by Dawna De Silva

If you enjoyed this book, please check out these other works by Dawna De Silva.

SOZO
Saved, Healed, and Delivered: A Journey into Freedom with the Father, Son, and Holy Spirit

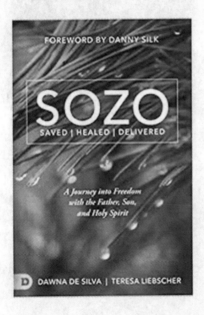

"In *SOZO*, Dawna De Silva and Teresa Liebscher provide revelatory teaching and miraculous testimonies that paint a stunning picture of how to experience Heaven's freedom in every area of your life."

Shifting Atmospheres:
Discerning and Displacing the Spiritual
Forces Around You

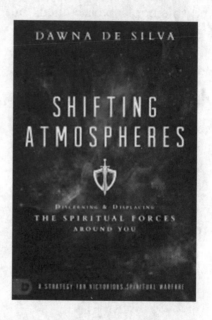

"Dawna De Silva presents a strategy for spiritual victory. Get ready to discern the enemy's tactics and learn how to use your weapons of warfare to enforce Jesus's victory over forces that war against your mind, your family, and your region!"

Overcoming Fear:
The Supernatural Strategy to Live in Freedom

"With practical and activating steps, Dawna De Silva, founder and coleader of the International Bethel Sozo Ministry, shows you how to battle anxiety, stress, and panic."

OTHER BOOKS

The Book of Healing:
A Journey to Inner Healing Through the
Book of Job

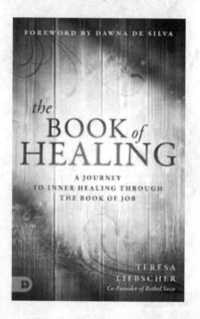

"Traditionally, the Book of Job is read as an account of suffering. But Teresa Liebscher, cofounder of Sozo, invites you to see this ancient biblical text as an invitation to powerful inner healing through defeating the enemy's lies and maintaining strong connection with God."

Money and the Prosperous Soul:
Tipping the Scales of Favor and Blessing

"In a warm, conversational style, CFO and CPA firm owner Stephen K. De Silva offers a unique, prophetic/supernatural approach to handling money. This respected charismatic leader combines financial philosophy, biblical truth, supernatural deliverance, and prophetic teaching, and also offers related practical and prophetic exercises throughout each chapter."

TEACHINGS BY STEPHEN DE SILVA

Prosperous Soul Master Course

"Don't stay stuck in the financial roller coaster of getting ahead only to fall behind. Take the journey of a Prosperous Soul. Walk out of poverty, fear, and lack and step into a new story defined by prosperity, abundance, and hope for you and your family!"

https://member.stephenkdesilva.com/
prosperous-soul-masterclass

Prosperous Home Master Course

"Don't stay stuck in your financial pattern. Get the momentum and tools you need to accomplish your financial goals. Build the foundation you want and create a Prosperous Home for you and your family!"

https://member.stephenkdesilva.com/ prosperous-home-master-course30162971

MORE RESOURCES

If you would like to access more teachings from Dawna De Silva or Stephen De Silva, visit Dawna's product page at https://shop.bethel.com/search?q=dawna+de+silva or Stephen's at https://stephenkdesilva.com/store.